Once Saved... Always Saved

Perry Lassiter

BROADMAN PRESS
Nashville, Tennessee

All Scripture quotations are from the
Revised Standard Version unless otherwise indicated.

Library of Congress Catalog Card Number: 74-15289

Dewey Decimal Classification: 234

Printed in the United States of America

Contents

TO

Vivian

who perseveres with me

Introduction

"Can you recommend a book on perseverance, predestination, and petitionary prayer?"

The young lady approached me with this question after a prayer meeting discussion on perseverance. When I recovered from the alliteration, I picked myself up and told her I doubted it. Later I did a little research and found almost no book on perseverance at all, much less combined with the other two "p's."

I therefore took the research I had done for the prayer meeting series, dug a little deeper, and began putting it on paper. Predestination *is* discussed in here, but the book she asked for will have to wait awhile.

Most of the significant Bible verses are quoted in the book for the reader's convenience. He would do better, however, to read with Bible in hand to examine the full passage. Two or more translations also help in some of the stickier passages.

Except where the context plainly shows otherwise, "once-saved-always-saved" is synonymous with "perseverance of the saints," "perseverance," "security of the believer," and "security." Any one of these words may also be shorthand for "the doctrine of perseverance" or "those who believe in the doctrine of perseverance." The context usually makes this clear.

Likewise the following are generally synonymous as I use them in this book: "apostasy," "falling from grace," and "losing your salvation." It should be noted that I use the term "apostasy" most often to refer to the doctrine that one may be saved and then lost. I do this for convenience only. The reader may see in Chapter 5 how I think the term should properly be used.

1
The Nature of the Question

Can a man lose his salvation?

Many Christians have asked this question, some with deep concern. And this is good, for even discussing the issue throws a good deal of light not only on the topic itself, but also on a number of related subjects, such as the nature of salvation, faith, and God's dealings with man. The exploration begins with the question itself.

It is always useful to ask questions. It is *most* useful to ask questions clearly and precisely. A well-stated question is halfway to the answer. Yet sometimes expressing the problem can be the most difficult part of the quest. This is true in the present case of the security of the believer, or the "perseverance of the saints," or "once-saved-always-saved." The surface questions must give way to a deeper question.

The Surface Question

"Pastor, tell us why we believe you can't fall from grace."

"Is it true you can accept Christ and go on living in sin?"

"I could never be a Baptist. I just don't believe that once you're saved, you're always saved."

Any Baptist or Presbyterian pastor hears questions or

statements like these often. They arise from the traditional stance of the two denominations in teaching that a Christian is eternally secure and can never again be lost. But this is a minority opinion, and the bulk of the denominations do not accept this doctrine.

We thus have a serious responsibility to be sure of our ground when we go against the mainstream of Christian thought. But we also have an obligation to seek out the truth regardless of the weight of opinion. We have stood firm in our insistence on believer's baptism over the years, and now the other confessions are moving in our direction.

Perhaps the simplest way to state the question is: "If a man is once saved, can he ever be lost?"

Now in many people's minds this question really means something like this—can John Doe have a single religious experience at 11:55 A.M. on January 1, 1974, and then die on January 1, 1999, and still go to heaven regardless of what happens in between?

To be perfectly honest, I can only answer that question in *two* ways—first theoretically, then practically. I would first have to say yes, this is a theoretical possibility, provided it is the right kind of experience. Just as quickly I would say that, practically speaking, this is not very likely if there are no other evidences of salvation.

The question itself is stated poorly. It implies only a partial view of salvation, limiting it to a future state of bliss in heaven. For some salvation becomes a kind of one-payment insurance policy with heaven as the pay-off. It implies that one act of decision here is all that is required for eternity.

Strictly speaking, this is true, but taken by itself this

view is too narrow. It is rather like looking at the one-foot width of a brick wall and then stepping out to see that it is ten feet long!

A Closer Look

Salvation is an encounter with the living Christ in which the Holy Spirit calls a person, the person says yes, and God changes the person's life.

This experience is so tremendous and so radical that the Bible compares it to being born again and speaks of the person as a new creature. The Spirit enters his life and he can never again be the same. All of his life is conditioned by that event just as all of life is conditioned by physical birth.

As Baptists, we have often overreacted to groups who add this, that, and the other to the biblical plan of salvation.[1] In denying (rightly) these other things we have often shrunk salvation down to a very small size in the minds of many people. We preachers are particularly guilty of emphasizing that we are saved by "mere" faith or "mere" grace.

And that we are, but faith and grace are not so mere! Very powerful indeed they are, and when a man lets God loose in his life, drastic things start to happen.

An Improved Question

So when we ask whether if we are once saved we can ever be lost, let us underline the word *saved*. We are raising the question only about those who have had a genuine encounter with Christ and whose lives have been changed by the power of God. This leaves out a number of people:

• We are not talking about just anyone who has had a religious experience. Buddhists, Hindus, pagans have these. LSD gives experiences that users describe as religious. An emotional experience in a Christian church may not be a salvation experience even if it is in some other way religious.

• We are not talking about someone who has walked down an aisle, or joined a church, or was baptized. Christians have done this, but having done this does not insure the person is a Christian.

• We are not talking about someone who has lived a good moral life. Paul did this before his conversion and maintained afterward that it was worthless (Phil. 3:4-8).

We are discussing in these pages only those who have been genuinely converted to real discipleship. This removes from consideration those who are in the categories listed above.

Do you begin to see how examining the question more closely clarifies the problem? Now let's hack away at some more underbrush in the second half of the question.

Back to the Surface

". . . is he always saved?"

Again this question is popularly interpreted to mean only whether he will go to heaven when he dies. And again I would have to answer personally yes if he has had a genuine salvation experience but that I doubt it if the only evidence you have is that he walked down an aisle. And again I would suggest we try and reframe the question at a deeper level.

Salvation includes more than going to heaven. First

of all, it makes one a fit citizen for heaven. It has been characterized as having three stages: past, present, future.

In the past stage "salvation" refers to conversion, the act of commitment to Christ that began the Christian life and secured the forgiveness of sins. A provocative question at this point might be: If a man *could* lose his salvation, would it mean that God no longer forgives him for the sins before his conversion, or is he held accountable only for those sins after his apostasy? Or is it possible that man's forgiveness includes not only the past, but future sins from the time that he makes his surrender to Christ?

In the present stage "salvation" refers to the process of Christian growth toward maturity. It is the continuing action of God in a person's life. It is what the Bible calls the "fruit of the Spirit" or, in James, "works." [2]

One modern-day theologian insists that we are all only "Christians in the making." This recognition would alter our question to include asking whether if a man is saved, does God always continue to work in his life?

In the future stage "salvation" refers to the consummation of the Christian life with God in heaven for eternity. It is everlasting life and eternal life. While this is perhaps the most commonly understood stage of salvation, it should be pointed out that Bible scholars have almost all emphasized that eternal life begins not after death, but immediately upon salvation. "Eternal" is a word that speaks of a kind of life, not primarily of length of life as "everlasting" does. In salvation the eternal breaks into time here and now, but its fullness awaits the "Day of the Lord," the return of Christ, or heaven.

Thus, we might summarize the last half of this question

by making sure that it includes a *full* view of salvation.
If we are once saved, does that experience insure forever
our forgiveness of all sins and that God will continue
working in our lives, bringing us to maturity until he
calls us to be with him forever?

Put It All Together And . . .

Now let's look again at the original question and its
expansion. If a man is once saved, is he always saved?
Remembering our discussion, let's ask it again like this:
If God once breaks into a man's life confronting him
with his Son Jesus Christ, so that the man says yes to
God and opens his life for the Spirit to come in and
remake that man's life, will God continue to forgive that
man and lead him to grow in grace and service, regardless
of what happens, until he calls him home to heaven?

Of course, this gives us a long, run-on, and confusing
sentence as precise questions tend to be, but it can be
broken down like this:

If these things happen:

> God calls a man,
>
> the man encounters Christ,
>
> the man says "yes" and surrenders his life,
>
> the Holy Spirit enters his life and changes it so
> that he is born again, a new creature;

Will these things then happen:

> the man will always be forgiven,
>
> God will always work in him for growth and
> maturity,
>
> God will take him to heaven when he dies;
>
> Regardless of what (else) happens in between?

To clarify this a bit more, let's put the last half negatively:

If the above things happen, is there *any* way
> he can lose his forgiveness,
> prevent God's continuing to work in his life,
> lose his claim to heaven and end in hell?

Things Are Simplified

Put like this, the question becomes much easier to handle. We know we are dealing only with genuinely saved people now and asking whether they can become unsaved. We are also talking about the full range of salvation and not merely the last part of it. This is still a very difficult question, and sincere Christians will continue to disagree about the answer. But perhaps we can now think more clearly about that answer.

Notes

1. Compare our overreaction to the treatment of the Lord's Supper as a sacrament. In avoiding this we often reduce it to a brief ritual tacked on to the end of the worship service. Likewise with the doctrine of the Holy Spirit. In our fear of "tongues" we avoid any mention of the Spirit.

2. Cf. Galatians 5:16 ff., James 2:14-26, 1 John 3:1-10.

2
The Bible and Perseverance

Introduction: How to Interpret the Bible

Before we jump in and look at what the Bible says about perseverance, let's consider some of the rules for interpreting the Bible. This will give us a sort of yardstick to evaluate the pros and cons of the argument.

Rule One

What *exactly* does the Bible say?

This sounds very obvious, but it is perhaps the most neglected rule of biblical interpretation. For example, Who tempted Adam and Eve? Most people will answer "the devil" or "Satan," but this is not what Genesis says. It says the serpent tempted Eve. Now I think the serpent was Satan or at least an emissary of his, but this is my deduction—probably a true one, but still only a deduction. It is *not* what Genesis says.

So whenever we study the Bible seriously, we must try to clear our minds of what we *think* the Scriptures say and make sure of exactly what they do say—no more and no less. This is especially important for our question of the security of the believer because there are a number of passages that some feel imply a man can again be lost after being saved. But there is no Scripture passage that explicitly states that a man can be saved and then lose that salvation and go to hell. And, to be fair, neither is there a passage that says in so many words that a person who has once been saved can never, under any circumstances lose that salvation. But I feel that there are some that come very close to saying this.

Rule Two

What does the passage or verse mean in context?

This should be a familiar principle to most readers. It simply means that you interpret the Scripture passage in light of what comes before and after the particular verse or verses in question and also in light of the historical and literary background of the book. This is where commentaries and the like come in.

But a great deal can be accomplished by simply backing up a few paragraphs and reading straight through the whole section that contains the part under study, including several verses beyond it. For example, we get the name "Lucifer" for the devil from Isaiah 14:12. If, however, we back up and read the whole chapter, we find that the reference is not to the devil but to the king of Babylon (v. 4). Again it may be implied (and has been) that the agency behind the king is the devil, but if so, it is *only* implied and the exact statement is a reference to the sins of the Babylonian king.

Rule Three

Don't explain passages away so they have no meaning at all. If it does not mean what our opponents say it means, what does it mean?

Often difficult Scripture passages have been carefully handled so that it can be seen that they do not indeed mean you can fall from grace, but in so doing they have been stripped of all positive meaning. Each verse is there

for a purpose. The author had something in mind when
he wrote it. What does it mean?

Rule Four

Harmonize the passage with other Scripture passages,
especially within the same book or within books by the
same author.

This means that we believe the Bible does not contra-
dict itself, especially on major doctrines. Harmonize first
with teachings elsewhere in the same book, then with
other writings by the same man (if there are any). Then
fit the idea in with the rest of the New Testament, paying
particular attention to the words of Jesus. There should
also be a positive relation to the Old Testament, for the
same God is revealed there.

At this point it is useful to remember that we generally
think in a Greek rather than in a Hebrew sort of way.
The Greek way is to work out a statement that is very
carefully balanced to consider all conditions. We might
want to say, for instance, that every time I open my
hand the ball will fall to the ground unless I am outside
a gravitational field, in which case the ball will float or
drift. A Hebrew might prefer to make two statements:
"I open my hand and the ball falls. I open my hand and
the ball floats." The two Hebrew sentences stand together
in tension, pulling against each other, but describing in
a different way the same truth as our statement.

Thus we can read in 1 John 1:8: "If we say we have
no sin, we deceive ourselves, and the truth is not in us."
Then we go right on to read in 3:6: "No one who abides
in him sins; no one who sins has either seen him or known
him." So too can we have verses that imply apostasy
and those that imply perseverance. Harmonizing them

is part of our task.

Rule Five

After all this, make deductions and applications. But do this only after observing the preliminaries and only by clearly defining deductions and applications as such.

Now deductions are necessary. They answer questions we ask that were not being asked in the first century. They enable us to apply the Scripture to our lives in the twentieth century. It is not enough to know only what the Bible meant to those who first read it. We must also know what it says to us. As modern scholars like to put it: "First find out what it meant, then find out what it means."

The New Testament and Perseverance

For the Christian the most important basis to decide any issue is the New Testament teaching. We shall look at various passages that relate to this doctrine. For convenience I have divided them into two sections: those I would call the chief statements of the doctrine and the statements I would call secondary. There are many more passages that might have been included in addition to, or even instead of, those that are here. Some selection must be made, however, and this is mine. (I do allude to some other Scripture passages, however.)

1. *The Chief Passages*

Galatians 3:1-5 ff.   "O foolish Galatians! . . . Let me ask you only this: Did you receive the Spirit by works of the law, or by hearing with faith? Are you so foolish? Having begun with the Spirit, are you now ending with the flesh? Did you experience so many things in vain?—if

it really is in vain. Does he who supplies the Spirit to
you and works miracles among you do so by works of
the law, or by hearing with faith?"

To me this passage is the most important in the New
Testament on the issue of perseverance because it comes
closest to dealing directly and consciously with the subject. Most other passages are aimed in another direction,
and the implications may or may not fairly represent
the author's view on the subject of perseverance.

Paul is writing to a group of Christians in a church
or several churches to combat a young heresy that was
trying to seduce the churches to a different kind of Christianity, one that was Jewish and legalistic.

Paul had preached salvation through personal encounter with Christ—grace on the part of God meeting
faith on the part of man. Now the "Judaizers" came
agreeing with Paul—up to a point. Paul was correct, they
said, as far as he went. But he didn't go far enough. You
must also add the good works of the Jewish law or you
were not truly saved. You must submit to the rite of
circumcision and observe the fast days and otherwise keep
the whole gamut of Jewish laws.

Opposing this with all his might, Paul wrote the letters
to the Romans and the Galatians. Both are devoted largely
to insisting that one is saved by grace and faith alone—
without the works of Jewish legalism.

In Galatians 3 Paul uses this reasoning. How did you
start the Christian life, by faith or works? God obviously
has blessed you. You have already had an outpouring of
the Spirit. Did he do this through Jewish legalism?

The answer is obviously no. Paul had used a similar
argument at a church conference in Jerusalem and Peter

upheld him with reference to his own experiences at Caesarea (Acts 15:8; cf. 11:15-17). When they related how God has poured out his Spirit and converted the Gentiles, the other apostles were glad and imposed no other requirements.

Remember that at this time these people had no New Testament except, possibly, some sayings of Jesus that were being circulated orally or written. So Paul appeals not to Scripture but to their experience, like this:

You believed.

God blessed you and continues to bless you.

Why add anything?

This is what Paul meant around A.D. 55 when he wrote Galatians.

What does this have to do with perseverance? Just about everything. Consider:

It is generally agreed that we are saved by grace, through faith. But "falling from grace" almost always carries with it the idea that we lose our salvation through acts of sin. In other words, we are converted by the power of God but must continue in our own power. We are saved by grace, but must continue by works.

Paul is specifically rejecting that idea here. True, he is saying this in answer to another problem, yet his answer can be given quite intelligibly to our problem. Watch:

Paul, after God saves us, can we do something to lose our salvation?

Let me ask *you* only this: Did you receive the Spirit by the works of the law or by hearing with faith? Are you so foolish? Having begun in the Spirit, are you now ending with flesh?

I believe it is in keeping with the spirit and almost

the letter of Paul's statements to apply the passage to the security of the believer by making some statement such as the following:

Because God saves us by grace and we begin the Christian life by faith, we must beware of changing the rules and trying to continue the Christian life in our own strength through good works. If we fail in our good works and lapse into sin, this would mean we lost our salvation, even if we substitute Baptist good works of the twentieth century for Jewish good works of the first century. Thank God our salvation does not depend on our ability to hold out. We persevere the same way we began—by grace, through the power of God's Spirit in faith.

John 6:37-40,44,50—*Jesus' strongest statement on this topic.* "All that the Father gives me will come to me; and him who comes to me I will not cast out. For I have come down from heaven, not to do my will, but the will of him who sent me; and this is the will of him who sent me, that I should lose nothing of all that he has given me, but raise it up at the last day. For this is the will of my Father, that everyone who sees the Son and believes in him should have eternal life; and I will raise him up at the last day. No one can come to me unless the Father who sent me draws him; and I will raise him up at the last day. This is the bread which comes down from heaven; if any one eats of this bread he will live forever."

Jesus was drawing a parallel between his ministry and that of Moses, using manna as an illustration. He had fed five thousand the day before, and they had returned the very next day. Jesus challenged their motives, accusing them of coming only for the material reward of bread.

He said in effect: "No physical food today boys, only
spiritual. Not food for your bodies but food for your souls.
And the spiritual food is that which God gives, the bread
of life—and I am that bread."

And then he goes on in the sort of discourse that John
alone of the Gospel writers likes to record. Part of that
discourse is printed above. This was, of course, an evange-
listic address, but his statements tell heavily for the security of those who accept his message. Listen again:

"If you come to me I will not cast you out—I will
not refuse you." In the original Greek, there is a double
negative, two "no's" for emphasis. One of these is a
conditional word which means that I will not refuse you
or cast you out provided that you come to me. The other
is an absolute word which means in no case would I do
that. Together they make a *very* strong negative.

Now Jesus probably spoke Aramaic, not Greek. One
word which could have been translated here by "cast
out" is derived from a word meaning "street," thus giving
the idea that if you take refuge with me, I will never
under any circumstances throw you out into the street.

It's hard to get any more secure than that!

He makes the statement doubly strong by referring it
to God's eternal will that no one should be lost who comes
to him. And he confirms it by a kind of musical refrain
running several times through the discourse: "and raise
him up at the last day." This repeated refrain in itself
is an assurance of security.

Now doesn't this virtually answer our question about
perseverance? We must admit that Jesus is not quite
putting it in our words so that it would leave the answer
absolutely unequivocal, but he comes so very close to

it! It should take very strong evidence—which I don't
know about—to make it mean otherwise.

Jesus is saying that if you come to me, God intends
for me to keep you. Therefore, I will indeed keep you
safe under all circumstances, even to the point of raising
you from the dead.

If that's not security, I don't know what is!

John 17:11,12,20—*the high priestly prayer.* "Holy Father, keep them in thy name, which thou hast given me,
. . . While I was with them, I kept them in thy name,
which thou hast given me; I have guarded them, and
none of them is lost but the son of perdition, that the
scripture might be fulfilled. . . . I do not pray for these
only, but also for those who believe in me through their
word."

John 17 is known as the high priestly prayer. It is a
prayer of Jesus for his disciples at the conclusion of the
Lord's Supper, just before he goes out to be arrested and
crucified. Among other things, he says in this prayer that
he has kept the disciples and is now entrusting them into
the keeping of his father. In verse 20 he refers to those
who will become disciples in the future through the
testimony of these eleven, and he asks God to bless them
in the same way he is asking God to bless the eleven.
He says quite specifically that none of the twelve has
been lost except Judas. (We'll talk about Judas later.) This
sounds very much like perseverance—and not in their
own strength. He does not say that they have endured,
or remained faithful, or continued to follow. Rather he
says *he has kept them.*

Then he entrusts them into his Father's hands and asks
him to continue to keep them. In verse 20 he opens the

request to include the future believers, which is where we come in. We, too, are to be made one with the first disciples and kept, not by our own power, but by his.

And now about Judas. Because someone has exclaimed: "Aha! You skipped him. Isn't he an example of falling from grace?"

Yes, he is—*if* you believe that Judas was at one time a committed believer, and this is highly debatable. In fact, this passage by itself makes it rather difficult to put him in the same category as the other disciples. It calls him a "son of perdition" and classifies his action as fulfilling the Scripture. Other passages call him a thief.

Personally, I feel that Judas was never a sincere disciple as the others were. Judas misunderstood from the beginning. I think of him as a member of one of the zealot bands looking for an earthly messiah who would be a militant guerilla leader. Like Judas Maccabeus had done two hundred years before, the messiah would overthrow the foreigners and Israel would again be free, perhaps even the leading nation in the world! Judas Iscariot fixed on Jesus as the man most likely to succeed in rallying the people to his cause.

When this did not happen and Jesus did not seem to be interested in being this kind of messiah, Judas betrayed him, either in disgust or in hopes that Jesus' arrest would cause a popular uprising and force Jesus to act as a military leader. Many modern Bible scholars think this may have been in Judas' mind. In fact the other disciples occasionally reflected similar ideas, but their commitment to Jesus was more open to his teaching. They, too, ran away, and Peter denied him; but they all came back. Judas did not, and that makes all the difference. He did not come back because he had nothing to come back to. It was not in his nature.

To some this may seem like special pleading or stacking the cards. As a matter of fact, however, very few would classify Judas as ever having been a Christian. And if he never had been saved, he could not lose his salvation.

• *A note on the passages in John.* I have put a good deal of weight here on Jesus' words in the book of John. A few readers may question this since it is very difficult at times to separate the exact words of Jesus from the words of the author. There is one school of thought that believes the "discourses" (long speeches) in John are so different in style that they could not have been spoken by the same man who said the things recorded in the first three Gospels.

Perhaps the best reply to these critics would be that whether these were the *ipsissima verba* of Jesus or not, they are obviously sayings which the author felt were consistent with what Jesus did say. Further, they were sufficiently consistent with other Christian teachings to be accepted by the church as canonical.

I have also not been convinced by the argument that differences in style mean that Jesus must have said one or the other, but not both. A man as outstanding as Jesus (even in the merely human sense) must easily have been capable of more than one style of speech. Perhaps the Synoptic Gospels relate his more usual style of speech while John records a more intimate style, used most frequently within the circle of the twelve. I also like the view that one purpose of John was specifically to include material not preserved in the other Gospels.

Most readers will not be bothered by this problem since

for them the Scripture would be true simply because it is in the Bible, regardless of who spoke it.

2. *Other Important Passages*

Mark 4:1-9—*the parable of the sower.* Jesus describes a gardener, walking down a path and "broadcasting" seed in all directions. What becomes of the seed depends entirely upon the kind of ground on which it falls. It is known as the parable of the sower, but a parable of the soils would more accurately describe it. For the basic teaching of the story is that the same messenger and the same message will produce widely different reactions, depending on the hearer. One particular application is to the ministry of Jesus and those who heard him.

In one important way this parable differs from others. Most parables have one and only one central meaning. A Bible student should always seek out that central point first. And in most cases it is dangerous to go beyond that main point to draw conclusions because that is not what the parable was designed for. In this case, however, Jesus himself interprets the parable, at least partly, as an allegory and identifies at least four kinds of "soils" or listeners. The first group are pretty clearly those who never become Christians and are never considered as such. The last group seem equally obviously to be Christians. Neither have much to do with our study of perseverance.

The two middle groups, however, are very interesting. What you decide about these groups has much to do with your position on apostasy and security. Jesus speaks of one kind of man who hears the word and responds well at first but fades under pressure. Another group has the word choked out by weeds. In one sense, the second group is pictured as enduring for awhile and then falling away. Yet both in the story and the explanation the first three groups are really lumped together. Jesus gives approval only to the last group, and it is only the last group that brings forth fruit.

I believe that Jesus is pointing out that there are many ways to receive the gospel, but only one right way. The other ways are not genuine and do not last even though men may not always be able to distinguish between them. Thus, in our discussion of perseverance this gives us biblical grounds to say that Jesus himself distinguished between committed believers and those who were merely curiosity seekers or on an emotional binge or "religious kick." Referring to our original statement of the problem, this reminds us that in our discussion of security of the believer we are talking only about the last of these "soils." It also confirms our experience that there are indeed some who only appear to receive the gospel but do not do so in depth or reality.

Matthew 20:1-16—*The parable of equal wages.* The more I think about this parable, the more I become convinced that it has much to teach us, perhaps because it is relatively ignored. Part of its relevance bears directly on perseverance.

The story tells of a man who hired laborers for his farm. He begins early in the morning and makes three other trips to town during the day and adds men at each trip. Instead of paying by the hour, he settles with them at the end of the day by paying all of them the same full day's wage he agreed on with the early morning crew. When that worthy group complained, he answered that he had treated them justly as they agreed on. If he wished to be generous and pay the other workers the same amount, this was his privilege. And Jesus said the kingdom of heaven is like that.

People often wonder about deathbed repentance. Can a man repent at the very last minute and still be forgiven? It is tempting to answer that this is the whole point of the parable. The eleventh-hour workers received the same reward as those who had worked all day. The wage for one hour equaled the wage for twelve hours. And Jesus in his economy felt this was just, even generous. He had paid all he had agreed on and more.

By inference this can also relate to perseverance. If God rewards the man who worked one hour at the end of the day, might he not also reward the man who worked an hour or two early in the day and then quit?

Yes, this does go against our feelings of what is just, but the New Testament is first of all a book about mercy and salvation. It might indeed be more just and fair for God to desert one who deserts him, but this is the whole thrust of the New Testament. Indeed, God sent his Son to save us while we were yet sinners. How much more would he be willing to forgive us who have begun to follow that Son (cf. Rom. 5:8-10).

The parable also moves to judge our own judgmental attitudes. Why does God do things the way he does? Why doesn't he reward me more and others less? Why should he reward one who repents on his deathbed or commits apostasy as much as he does me—I have been faithful all the time? This is often our attitude. It is exactly the feeling of the elder brother in the story of the prodigal son.

It is not really any of our business why God is gracious

to others. We need only be grateful that he is gracious
to us. We need also to remember Jesus' comment to
Peter at the end of the Fourth Gospel. Jesus had prophe-
sied to Peter some of what would happen to him, and
Peter then asks what is going to happen to John? In effect,
Jesus says to him, "What I want John to do is none of
your business. You take care of Peter. You see that you
follow me."

Matthew 18:21-22—*forgiveness: 70 times 7.*   Peter felt
he had become very liberal and was really catching on
to Christ's teachings. So there may have been some brag-
gadocio in his manner as he asked Jesus, "How many
times should I forgive my brother when he sins against
me? Is seven times enough?" Jesus' answer deflated him:
"Not seven times, man, seventy times seven."

And Jesus didn't mean to keep score.

In the version in Luke the disciples cry out in pain
at Jesus' answer, "Lord, increase our faith!" And well
they might. What man can live up to this?

But God does.

God repeatedly forgives us. If he lays this command
on us, he does so because it is in his nature to forgive.
God asks nothing of us that he himself does not possess
in far greater measure. From the cross Christ cried out
"Forgive them."

Now this obviously applies to perseverance and
thoroughly dynamites the argument that says you lose
your salvation through only one or even a few sins. It
may leave open the question of whether there is some
immense quantity of sins or particularly evil sins that
might lead eventually to divine rejection. But it very
clearly means that if God expects us to forgive one an-

other, he will set the example.

John 2:23; 1 John 4:1-3—*further evidences of a shallow, nonsaving faith.* The parable of the soils gave us the clearest example that Jesus did not feel that all faith was saving faith. There are other Scripture passages that reinforce this idea and so support our argument that many cases of apostasy are only a fall from shallow faith, not the life-changing faith of genuine conversion.

Jesus makes a tremendously important judgment that John records in 2:23 f. Many believed in him, but he did not believe in them. The Revised Standard Version says, "he did not entrust himself to them." It is the same Greek word in both instances, but in different tenses.

The first word "believed" is expressed in such a way (the aorist tense) that it indicates action for an instant with little or no duration: they only believed for a moment, or they were only beginning to believe. Jesus recognized that this was not much faith—a shallow soil type of thing that would spring up but soon wilt.

John may have remembered this later when he wrote the little letter we call 1 John. In it he says, "Do not believe every spirit, but test the spirits." Not everyone who claims to be a believer is one. Neither is everyone who claims to speak for God a true prophet. And not every message that claims to come from God is in fact from him. So test the spirits, try out the prophets, examine their messages. Not all is genuine.

And this means that some apparent cases of apostasy are merely revelations of what the true state has been all along. They are not examples of falling from grace, but revelations of never having been in a state of grace at all. And this leads us into the next section.

The faith and works controversy. The book of James has been a source of great tension in the church because the author says that faith without works is dead (Jas. 2:17). Many have said this is a flat contradiction of Paul, who says a man is saved only by grace and faith without works. Some have approached the controversy by pointing out that Paul and James meant different things by "works." While this may be true, I am convinced there is another approach.

The faith and works controversy is based on a phony issue. *All* the biblical writers agree and insist that faith, if it is genuine, will demonstrate itself in the life of the individual.

Paul in his letter to the Galatians is arguing specifically for the thesis that one is saved by grace without the works of the law. Yet he says specifically in this very book also (5:19 ff.) "Now the works of the flesh are plain: immorality, impurity, licentiousness, idolatry, sorcery, enmity, strife, jealousy, anger, selfishness, dissension, party spirit, envy, drunkenness, carousing, and the like. I warn you, as I warned you before, that those who do such things shall not inherit the kingdom of God. But the fruit of the spirit is love, joy, peace, patience, kindness, goodness, faithfulness, gentleness, self-control; against such there is no law. And those who belong to Christ Jesus have crucified the flesh with its passions and desires."

Paul is saying in different words exactly the same thing as James. The same idea recurs throughout the book of 1 John and in the teachings of Jesus ("Why do you call me 'Lord' and don't practice what I preach?").

Now, back to the main subject. What does all this have to do with the security of the believers? As we've said before, it again underscores the fact that there are groups of people, identified with Christianity, who do not in fact know Christ. They are only superficial believers. Some may go on to a life-transforming faith; others may fall away. But it is expected that a genuine Christian will give some evidence in his life.

Perhaps a practical warning should be inserted here. While it is biblical and good to speak this way in a general sense, it becomes dangerous to the point of sin to apply this to individuals. In other words, we should be very slow to say that so-and-so is not a Christian because we can't see it in his life. Matthew 7:1-2 warns us against this sort of thing. Besides, the problem may be with my vision more than your life!

1 Corinthians 5:2,13—*Paul's advice on church discipline.*   The church at Corinth was a pastor's nightmare. If a preacher ever gets down in the dumps over his congregation, all he has to do is read 1 Corinthians and he'll begin to rejoice. *No* church could ever be *that* bad. Except that it was!

There were factions—many of them. There was speaking in tongues, jealousy, licentiousness, heresy—you name it and they had it. So it's not surprising to discover that Paul tells them to kick someone out: "Let him who has done this be removed from among you . . . drive out that wicked person from among you." What *is* surprising is that Paul only tells them to kick out one member. Out of all this fantastic array of problems, Paul singles out only one for excommunication. He did not choose the heretics. He did not recommend kicking out the tongues-speakers. He did not even command them to discipline the licentious. The only one he asked them

to discipline publicly was a man who was living with
his father's wife. He was doing this openly and making
the church a laughing stock even in the pagan world.
And even this was to be done in love and in order to
save the man (5:5).

"Well," someone may say, "he did order one kicked
out. Doesn't even one example prove apostasy?" Perhaps
so, but this isn't that example. This man apparently repented and was restored to fellowship in the church.
Second Corinthians 2:5-8 is almost certainly a plea for
the same man, who had repented, to be taken back in.

(Incidentally, this is quite a different ending from any
modern case of church discipline that I've heard about.
Usually the ejection communicates rejection, and the
person is lost forever to the church. Or else, it evolves
into a mass turn-out that results in a split and a second
church started down the road. The New Testament does
teach church discipline, but it is not quick on the trigger.
It is characterized by concern, and its aim is redemption,
not condemnation. Contrary to many modern heresy
hunters, Paul does not feel the heretics need to be thrown
out. He prefers to oppose them, withstand them, and
out-argue them. If he couldn't convince them, he left
them to God.)

This excursion into the discipline of the early church
bears on security in the following way. Paul feels there
is hope for even such a messed-up church as this and
for the people in it. He particularly feels there is hope
for the worst sinner in the crowd and points the way
to his redemption. He does not condemn the crowd as
lost and non-Christian. Rather he treats them as immature
Christians who need guidance to grow in grace.

Paul felt that most of these people were genuine Christians and he seems to have had full confidence that they would make it. And that, friends, is perseverance. And if the folks at Corinth persevered . . . , why the folks in your church will too!

2 Timothy 1:12. "For I know whom I have believed and am persuaded that he is able to keep that which I have committed unto him against that day" (KJV).

This has been the favorite passage for those who believe in perseverance. I have chosen to place it further down the list, however, because of a translation difficulty. Many modern translators feel the verse means that God is able to protect and defend the gospel message regardless of the persecution the messenger may have to undergo.

For example, the RSV translates, "He is able to guard until that Day what has been entrusted to me." Literally the expression is "my commitment." The phrase may be translated, "he has power to guard my commitment." This commitment may be either that which Paul has committed to God or that which God had committed to Paul. Both are live choices, and if the first translation is correct, we have a passage supporting perseverance very strongly.

It would also be possible to ride both horses and say the commitment refers to all that God has done with him including his salvation and his ministry. Looking at the verse in context, we see that Paul is telling Timothy not to be ashamed of the gospel or the persecution connected with it. Paul, himself, is not discouraged in the face of real suffering for he is sure that God will watch over his commitment.

If we interpret the commitment in any sense that would

include his salvation, the verse affirms Paul's belief that
he is secure in the hands of God regardless of what men
do to him. He does not here state that this confidence
extends to all believers but speaks only of himself. On
the other hand his confidence is not in himself, but in
God who will keep him. So there seems to be no reason
why the concept cannot be expanded to all who have
believed. When we commit our lives into the hands of
God, he keeps that which we entrust to him until that
day we meet him face to face.

Jude 24. "Now unto him who is able to keep you
from falling and to present you without blemish before
the presence of his glory with rejoicing."

The argument here is short and sweet. Matthew 18:14
says that God is not willing that even one should perish.
Add this to Jude 24 and you have a rather neat syllogism:

> God is able to keep us (Jude 24)
>
> God wants to keep us (Matt. 18:14)
>
> Therefore God *will* keep us.

It combines two unrelated passages. One is a benediction, not a theological passage. The logic is not conclusive.
But the idea haunts you. And it feels right.

Matthew 16:16—*Peter's denial of Christ.*   There are
two examples of apparent apostasy in the New Testament
in the life of the twelve Jesus chose. We've discussed
Judas a bit and will return to him in the next section.
Now let's look at Simon Peter.

Simon was a believer. He followed Jesus and made
all sorts of impulsive statements. Among these was perhaps the greatest confession of all—"Thou art the Christ,
the Son of the Living God" (Matt. 16:16). Tremendous.

And yet, not so very long afterwards the same lips

cursed and swore like the sailor Simon once was and said emphatically, "I do not know the man." Surely this was apostasy in the first degree.

But it is not the end of the story. Simon goes out and weeps bitterly. Then he goes to the open tomb; he sees the risen Christ. And Jesus meets him by the lake ("Do you love me?"). Simon is forgiven, restored, and a month later wins three thousand people with one sermon.

If a man can fall from grace, this should have done it. Instead, it became a stepping stone to strength. Simon, the denyer went on to become Simon, the Rock. And that's perseverance.

Philippians 1:6. "I am certain that he who began a good work in you will go on bringing it to completion until the day of Christ."

This is my personal favorite verse for preaching and individual encouragement, although I'm not sure that the scholarly argument from this verse is as strong as some of the others we have already cited.

Paul is speaking directly to the Philippians, one of his favorite congregations. He is saying that he is convinced that God will go on doing with them what they now see him doing until the day of Christ. He is saying that he believes they will persevere.

He does not, unfortunately, say that this is true of everyone. And yet, again he is not talking about what *they* are doing to persevere, but about what God is doing in them. So I like to tell parishioners, who worry about this sort of thing, that their very worry is a sign that God is at work in them and that he is going to continue working in their lives until that Day.

There is an interesting side effect to this approach,

by the way. I was recently talking with a young man who had not attended church for a couple of years although I had been told he was rather dedicated as a youth. I told him that since I believed in "once-saved-always-saved" I figured God would eventually lead him back into the church. To my surprise he agreed very quickly and (I thought) sincerely.

John 10:27-29—*The good shepherd.*   In answer to the question of the Pharisees about whether He is the Messiah, Jesus reminds them that he has already answered the question and they would not accept it. He characterizes himself as the good shepherd whose sheep recognize and follow him. If they had been among his flock, they would have known he was the Messiah and believed.

This statement reinforces our earlier argument about the nature of salvation. It is in the character of faith to follow; those who are not following have not believed.

Then Jesus goes on to promise those who are following him that he is giving them eternal life. Three times he asserts that they will never be lost:

They will never perish.

No one can snatch them from his hand.

No one can take them from the Father's hand.

The threefold emphasis certainly sounds like a believer is secure from anything. The Father is stronger than all, not just any one thing, but all things. Thus our security rests not on our ability to hold out, but on God's strength.

The word translated "snatch" here may have two senses. The first, and more usual Greek sense, is that of stealing or kidnapping. The second, and Hebrew sense, is that of an animal snatching to tear in pieces and devour. We are thus safe from kidnapping by those who would devour and destroy us.

Serious Bible students find a problem in the text of verse 29. The most reliable texts all read with the margin note of the RSV, "What my father has given me." Because this is hard to understand, most translators have read the Greek word "who" instead of "what" even in face of the evidence.

"What" would seem to refer to the church (sheep), and at the time of the writing the church was certainly not strong enough to bear the burden of protecting the believers. But William Barclay may have found a way out in his translation. He takes the "what" as referring to the power transmitted from the Father to the Son. This would tie in with the identity of the two as stated in verse 30. And it would mean that Jesus keeps the follower by the power that God has conferred upon him.

3. Summary of the New Testament Teaching

We have examined several lines of thought with direct bearing on the security of the believer.

• First, there are passages that remind us that we are not saved by works and that we do not continue by works. In other words, our perseverance, like our salvation, does not lie in our own hands, but in the hands of God.

• There are passages that speak directly of God's willingness and power to keep us. There are others that insist that we must rely on him and not ourselves.

• There are numerous miscellaneous passages that speak of God's forgiveness and his willingness to pay equal wages to all. There is this constant theme of including as many as possible rather than excluding.

• There are passages that speak of a shallow faith as

compared to a saving faith. This verifies our thesis that
not all who claim to be Christians are and, therefore,
at least some cases of apostasy are merely revelations
of the true condition of the individual all along.

One of the real problems in this survey has been decid-
ing which passages to include and which to omit. There
are many more which might have been included. Perhaps
most of these, however, have teachings similar to at least
one of the passages which have been discussed.

Overall, then, the New Testament strongly teaches that
Christians will be upheld by God's power and so persevere. We will consider some problems with this position
in the next chapter, but the problems are far outweighed
by the confidence of the Bible in God's saving power.

The Old Testament and Perseverance

I have reversed the usual order and postponed looking
at the Old Testament until now for two reasons. First
of all, I think it is more interesting this way. The New
Testament is fairly clear; the Old Testament provides
background. Second, the importance of the Old Testament
becomes more evident in our later discussion of theology
than for the arguments already studied.

In studying the Old Testament it is important not to
read back into it our understanding of the New Testament.
On the other hand, the God of Abraham is the same
as the God of Jesus and Paul. He has revealed himself
more fully in the later writings and therefore we find
a better understanding of him there. Yet the Old Testament should be consistent with the New, even if at
times it only gives a glimpse of what is more clearly
revealed in the New.

While the Old Testament presents the stories of many individuals, it is really the story of a people, the people of God, the nation Israel. Sadly, it is a nation that did not persevere, but it is a God who did. Let us see what we can discover about that perseverance from the Old Testament.

1. God's Covenants

The Old Testament reveals God as one who makes covenants. This is a chief characteristic of God and basic to understanding his actions. He relates himself to people through agreements or pacts.

In a sense, these are one-sided pacts. Man does not bargain with God. God is the stronger party, and he comes to man with the covenant he has already worked out. If you will do thus and so, he says, I will do this and that. If you fail in keeping the agreement, however, judgment will follow. Let's look at some chief examples.

• The formal idea of a covenant is not brought out until Abraham, but we see its roots as early as Adam and Eve and in Noah's rainbow. With Abraham we find the basic covenant on which the Jewish nation was later founded. Genesis 12, thus, is a key chapter in the Bible for it describes the giving of the covenant.

God comes to Abram and says: "Leave your country and your people and go to a land that I will show you. If you do this I will bless you, make your name great, and establish a nation from your descendents." Abram obeyed God, and God was faithful to him. His leaving and following God was the beginning of the Jewish race and nation. In one sense, it was the beginning of the story of the Bible and salvation.

• The second major covenant was made at Mount Sinai
when the Law was given. Many Bible scholars think of
this as the basic covenant since it was made with the
nation rather than just one man. I prefer to think that
the biblical understanding shows this as fulfilling the
original covenant with Abraham and opening the door
to higher fulfillment. It is an up-dating and expansion
of the earlier pact with Abraham. But it is true that this
is the founding of the nation; the Israelites themselves
enter the covenant. Abraham's call founded a race; Mount
Sinai founded a nation.

• Periodically, Israel is reminded of the covenant, and
at various stages in their national life a kind of renewal
takes place. One such key place is in the speech of Samuel
when Israel installs its first king. "And now behold the
king whom you have chosen, for whom you have asked;
behold, the Lord has set a king over you. If you will
fear the Lord and serve him and hearken to his voice
and not rebel against the commandment of the Lord,
and if both you and the king who reigns over you will
follow the Lord your God, it will be well;" (1 Sam.
12:13-14).

• The nation, however, rejects the covenant. Both they
and their kings fall from the worship of God and the
Lord therefore rejects them as a nation and race.

The Northern Kingdom falls first. When it splits from
the south, it sets up its own centers of worship at Bethel
and Dan instead of coming back to Jerusalem. Golden
calves are erected in these temples to represent God in
violation of the commandment against graven images.
Israel compounds this sin by permitting the worship of
foreign gods, the Baals. And so in 722 B.C. Israel fell

because she had not kept the covenant.

The southern state of Judah lasted longer, largely because it had only one center of worship and no graven images of the Lord. It was also more responsive to the warnings of the prophets, and the kings were more faithful to David's God. But they, too, permitted Baal worship from time to time and the erection of sacred poles or pillars, signs of the fertility cults. So Judah too fell.

• But even as these kingdoms fell, God was faithful to his promises. Indeed, he went beyond his promises. After Israel broke the original covenant, she no longer had claim to any of the promises of God. And God did bring the promised judgment, tempered with mercy.

There arose the idea of a remnant and a return, a faithful few who would remain and carry out the original covenant and mission of the nation. So even as judgment fell, the prophets continued to speak of the promises of God and of a remnant who would return and through whom God would fulfill his word.

God's covenant persevered in a most remarkable way. In that day it was assumed that when a nation was defeated, her gods were also defeated. Thus, the captives would turn to worship the superior foreign gods. Israel was the exception. By the waters of Babylon they sat down and wept, but they discovered they could sing the songs of their God in a strange land (Ps. 137). The Israelites, in captivity, found him to be not only the God of their little country, but of the whole earth. And when this remnant returned from captivity, they were guilty of many things, but never again were they guilty of idolatry or polytheism. They became fiercely monotheistic, worshipping only the one God (without idols), and focussing on the center at Jerusalem and on their sacred writings wherever they lived.

• In discussing the Old Testament, it is important to go beyond it to trace the covenant idea and the remnant idea. We have seen how all the people of God had shrunk to a small remnant. In the New Testament, we discover that the remnant itself has shrunk still smaller to only one man, Jesus Christ. He becomes the one of all Israel who is faithful to the calling and history of the nation. All of the covenants of God come to focus on him. And all the promises of God are fulfilled in him. In this one man on the cross, lonely between earth and sky, is the fulfillment of hundreds of years of promises. And as men believe on him and become a part of his new covenant, the remnant reverses and begins to expand. Now there is a new people of God, a new Israel, the church, and new covenants to fulfill.

So God's promise to Abraham still perseveres (cf. Gal. 3:6-29, esp. 29). In spite of the many infidelities of Israel, God remains faithful.

• A further note should be made here about the perseverance of Israel. I am not at all sure, personally, that the continued existence of the Jews or the development of the modern state of Israel is necessary to the fulfillment of prophesy. I believe that all the prophesies can be explained without that and that the new nation does not meet all the biblical criteria for such a nation.

Nevertheless, there it is. The Jewish people have miraculously survived. They have maintained their identity through all sorts of persecutions, absorptions, philosophies, and the ravages of time. Abraham's physical seed are still very much with us, and some are faithful to his beliefs.

Further, in 1948 the nation Israel was founded or refounded. It was established as a secular state, not a holy nation. And yet . . . there it is.

If this is not perseverance, it is strangely like it.

2. *The Choices of God*

Later on in our discussion the issue of predestination will have an important place. It is therefore important that we see that this idea also has its roots in the Old Testament.

God is always presented as a sovereign God, retaining his freedom of movement and choice. He will not be controlled or compelled. He creates the world with no explanation given. He simply chooses to do so. He chooses Abraham, and no explanation is given. He simply elects him. The same is true of Moses and many others.

God will work in his own way. Sometimes you can guess the reasons. Sometimes they are explained. But always there is a mystery about God and he retains the freedom to act as he chooses.

Abraham tried to help God out and Ishmael was born. But God preferred to carry out the covenant his own way and sent Isaac. He chose Jacob instead of Esau, and Joseph from among twelve brothers. He picked Solomon, child of Bathsheba, a marriage conceived in adultery and murder. God's answer to Job is perhaps the supreme expression of this in words. The choice of Israel from all the possible nations is the supreme example in deeds.

Much of the New Testament teachings rest on these and related ideas of the Old Testament. As we continue our study of perseverance, let's keep these in mind.

3
The Supposed Biblical Case Against Perseverance

Sincere critics of the doctrine of once-saved-always-saved turn to the Bible for support. And there are a number of passages that seem to give this support. We shall now look at these, remembering to be faithful to the rules previously set out for biblical interpretation. We shall be especially careful always to ask, If this doesn't mean loss of salvation, what *does* it mean?

The Chief Passages Used Against the Doctrine

Hebrews 6:4-8. "For it is impossible to restore again to repentance those who have once been enlightened, who have tasted the heavenly gift, and have become partakers of the Holy Spirit, and have tasted the goodness of the word of God and the powers of the age to come, if they then commit apostasy."

This is perhaps the passage of Scripture most commonly used in arguing that a person can lose his salvation. Since these verses seem so persuasive to many people, let us consider them carefully.

The obvious meaning for many is that Christians may indeed lose their salvation and fall from grace.

One popular interpretation is that the people in question are not in fact real Christians although they may seem to be. They are superficial believers whose faith

44

does not endure and so is proven false.

Another often used approach is to point out that this is a purely theoretical case he presents. He is not saying that apostasy is possible; he is saying only that *if* it is possible there is no repentance.

Herschel Hobbs suggests that the passage may refer to genuine apostasy, but only with regard to the present tense of salvation, not the past conversion nor future consummation. Thus, one may thwart God's will for him in present growth and service but not his ultimate purpose. Hobbs also points out that in verses 7-8 the land is burned, but it is the weeds that are destroyed.[1]

With these possible interpretations in mind, let us now look at the passage in the light of our basic principles of Bible study.

1. What does it say? To begin with the verse does not say that a person can lose his salvation, that he can lose the forgiveness of his sins from the time he was converted, or that the person in question will go to hell. It *does* say that it is impossible to restore such a one to repentance—and this is the only impossibility stated.

Second, the RSV translation is not reliable here since "commit apostasy" is an interpretation rather than a translation. While we may or may not be dealing with apostasy, the word used is one Greek word compounded of the word for "fall" with a prefix meaning "beside," "back," or "away." Thus it can mean to fall back, fall away, fall beside, or wander astray. A related Hebrew word means to act treacherously or to be unfaithful.

Note finally that in verse 9 the writer does say specifically that he does not believe these people have lost their

salvation or that they are going to lose it. On the contrary,
he goes on in verses 10-12 to emphasize that God will
not overlook their good works and love and urges them
to realize the full assurance of their hope until the end.

2. *What did it mean?*   For some reason, few commen-
tators take the time to link this difficult passage with
the rather clear passage that precedes it. The author has
been saying (5:11 to 6:3) that he would like to teach
the people some deeper truths of the faith but they are
too immature to understand these. Instead of growing
in grace, they have become stalled or frozen in their
development and have been repeating over and over again
to each other the elementary truths they were taught
when they first became Christians. The writer urges them
to let go of this shore and launch out to a deeper understanding of the gospel.

It is at this point that the difficult passage comes in.
The reason for leaving the first principles and going on
to maturity is that the people should by now have mastered the first ground. If they haven't, it is doubtful they
ever will. If they have mastered it and they lose it, they
are not likely to be brought back to repentance. *The words
of verses 4-8 are primarily an incentive for the readers
to become more mature in their Christian faith.* This is
the purpose and meaning of the verses. They are not
intended first of all as an exposition of either apostasy
or perseverance. Apostasy is discussed only secondarily,
and this should be kept constantly in mind. Because of
this it is risky to build a doctrine of any sort exclusively
on this verse or verses, especially if it conflicts with the
rest of the New Testament.

Now this cuts both ways. If apostasy had been the major

subject, the writer might have been more clear in either direction—toward the idea of perseverance (which I believe) or toward the idea that a man can lose his salvation (which some others believe). The New Testament position must be built up from the entire scope of the book and not from one or even a few passages.

3. An interpretation. Keeping in mind what the passage does and does not say and remembering the context, let us see what can be said about apostasy in Hebrews 6.

Let us begin with an often repeated, but valid, warning. *If* we interpret the passage to mean that apostasy involves loss of salvation, then the statement is quite clear that these newly-lost people have no hope of regaining salvation since repentance would be necessary and it is impossible to restore them to repentance. This excludes the beliefs of some Holiness groups that teach that a man can be saved and lost a number of times.

As a positive interpretation, I would make two points. First, I tend to agree with Hobbs that individual falling away would apply only to the present effects of salvation, not past forgiveness or future consummation. But I would also point out that the author here is not speaking of just any apostasy or backsliding. He is talking specifically about those who reject the basic, elementary teachings of the Christian faith. It is these, and only these, that he says cannot be restored to repentance. One reason for this is that such a person is *rejecting the very idea of repentance* (see v. 1). So long as they do this, of course they are not going to repent.

Now this means that, whatever else he is saying about apostasy, there may be other kinds of falling away that

are not covered here. For example, it may mean that
someone who lapses into sins of the flesh may be restored
to repentance as the Scripture elsewhere clearly teaches.
Indeed, even other forms of heresy may be brought to
repentance as the very existence of some of the Pauline
epistles imply.

Going a step further, I believe that the author here
is thinking more about a church or a group within the
church than individuals. He may be saying that a church
which goes off after a heresy that denies fundamental
beliefs is not going to be changed. For that matter, neither
is it likely for an individual who rejects such basic teaching. It is thus far better not to worry about these, wasting
time trying to restore them, but rather to expend the
church's major thrust on deepening the Christian life.

Finally, consider the situation of one who was genuinely
saved but later came to reject intellectually the basic
doctrines of salvation and even taught others this. In my
judgment he still has forgiveness of sins, and God will
receive him into heaven. Yet, he has very obviously
wrecked the possibility of winning others to Christ and
otherwise growing as a Christian. This, I believe, is what
this passage means.

Hebrews 10:26-31. "For if we sin deliberately after
receiving the knowledge of the truth, there no longer
remains a sacrifice for sins, but a fearful prospect of
judgment, and a fury of fire which will consume the
adversaries."

Once again let us note that this does not say that a
saved person may be lost, although it seems to come very
close to doing so. Indeed, it seems possible, at first reading,
that the verse might say that a deliberate sin after salva-

tion would send one to hell. The verse definitely does
not mean that.

A good part of the understanding of the verse hinges
on the meaning of "knowledge of the truth." In 1 Timothy
2:4 it is used parallel with "be saved" and in Titus 1:1
it is in a series of "faith, knowledge, and godliness." Since
the Hebrews liked to used expressions like this as syn-
onyms, it gives some weight to the belief that 10:26 means
saved people.

But this is not the only use of the word "knowledge."
(The non-Greek user is at a disadvantage as there are
several words translated with the English word "knowledge." *Gnosis* is more frequent, but this word is *epignosis*.
If you don't read Greek, *Young's Analytical Concordance*
breaks it down for the English reader. You can even see
the Hebrew equivalents of the Greek words.) In 2 Timothy
the word is used in opposition to the idea of correcting
opponents. The writer hopes these opponents will come
to "know the truth." Here the term "know" has more
of an intellectual quality to it although it includes the
hope that they would believe the truth as well as know
it. Paul goes on in 3:7 to talk about those who will listen
to anybody and can never arrive at a knowledge of truth.
Again, this seems to be as much intellectual knowledge
as commitment.

Second Peter 1:8 speaks of being ineffective or unfruit-
ful in the knowledge of Christ. Here the word is definitely
used as something separate from a life commitment.

Consequently, I would prefer to understand this word
epignosis here as meaning intellectual knowledge to the
point of mental understanding, but not necessarily to the
point of commitment or salvation.

What does it mean? I believe the author here is summing up his whole argument that the revelation of God in Christ is superior to all other revelations and that any attempt to tone it down or make it subordinate to anything else is heresy. It could be paraphrased like this: "If we deliberately continue sinning after having heard and understood the true way, the cross is of no value to us (because we have rejected it) and only judgment will follow."

It should also be pointed out that if apostasy *is* meant here, it does not involve merely a minor sin, however intentional. Verse 29 speaks of someone profaning the blood, spurning the Son, and outraging the Spirit. This is no less than gross heresy. In no case does this passage say one may lose his salvation for some light offense.

Verse 26 also says there is no longer any sacrifice left for these people, and verse 29 explains why: they have rejected the sacrifice and will not claim it. This does not sound like the actions of a converted man. The author, in fact, is sure that these people will not do this (v. 39).

In summary, the whole passage is directed at encouraging the new Christians to reject all heresies and hold fast to the faith they have been taught. The author is not primarily concerned with individuals wandering away, so much as he is with churches deserting the true doctrine. If this happens, the whole Christian faith is doomed, and this is why he writes with such passion. Even more is at stake than the eternal destiny of one or two or even a whole church of people. It involves the destiny of those who will hear in the future if the church is true to her calling. "Sin" in this case means the specific sin of heresy or the willingness to sin as a result of a heresy that says

it is all right for a Christian to sin. If we go on sinning
after all Christ has done to redeem us, then there is no
point to the faith.

No, I do not believe this is a threat that Christians
will lose their salvation. It is more a fear that the church
will lose its gospel.

2 Peter 2:20-22. "For if, after they have escaped the
defilements of the world through the knowledge of our
Lord and Savior Jesus Christ, they are again entangled
in them and overpowered, the last state has become worse
for them than the first. For it would have been better
for them never to have known the way of righteousness
than after knowing it to turn back from the holy commandment delivered to them. It has happened to them
according to the true proverb, The dog turns back to
his own vomit, and the sow is washed only to wallow
in the mire."

More than any other, this passage gives me trouble.
But the fact that a passage gives one trouble should not
be understood to mean that he has a guilty conscience
about twisting Scripture to say what he wants it to say.
The reason the passage gives trouble is that it is apparently
inconsistent with the whole weight of New Testament
evidence we have already considered. If we accepted this
verse to mean one could lose his salvation without close
examination, one of two things would follow. Either the
Bible is contradicting itself or we shall have to reexamine
all of the positive evidence, and this would *really* give
me trouble.

Fortunately, after considering all the pros and cons,
I really feel that this passage is also aimed at heretics
who are trying to spread their heresy to others. This

becomes more apparent if you back up and read the whole chapter. I would paraphrase it on this order: "If these people have just begun to extract themselves from their pagan society and before they get fully free find themselves again entangled, they are worse off than before. Previously they did it out of ignorance. Now they are deliberately choosing the old way after discovering there is another and better way."

Put that way it looks simple, doesn't it? But the problem comes from two words that would seem to be true of genuine Christians: "escaped" and the "knowledge" of Jesus. Some of the modern translations help us more clearly to see what may be meant by the idea of escaping. The Greek is such that the passage may be interpreted and even translated against the background of a pagan heritage. The "apostates" are just being converted from a rather wild and "heathenish" former state. They may have begun to follow the ethical teachings of Jesus before they had committed themselves to him.

This interpretation is furthered if you think of the word "knowledge" here as involving more intellectual understanding than personal commitment as we did in a section above. Thus, again, we have a case of seed falling on shallow soil. The pagans are attracted and investigate the new religion. They like parts of it but want to keep some of their old ways and ideas. So they try to mix them into the Christian teachings and lead church members to fall in with them. They have been thoroughly exposed to the truth, but turn back to their pagan ways, even if in some cases they keep the outward name and association of Christian.

It is totally possible that there are people who have

partially extracted themselves from a pagan background, but have not yet become bond-servants of Christ. Rather, they turn to some third choice, the heresy—in this case probably a Greek gnosticism that claimed the body could sin without tainting the soul.

Once more let's note that if these passages *do* refer to apostasy in the sense of losing one's salvation, these verses certainly are not claiming you can lose it through minor sins or even a good many major sins. It is again in the context of deliberate heresy and the attempt to lead others into heresy after having opportunity to know and understand the true way.

Other Important Passages

We have looked at three passages which, perhaps more than any others, trouble people and form the foundation of a doctrine of "falling from grace." But there are numerous other passages that, from time to time, seem to point in that direction just as there are numerous others that point toward security. Again, I have made a selection of a few of these that I feel are representative of all.

John 15:6. "If a man does not abide in me, and I in him, he is cast forth as a branch and withers; and the branches are gathered, thrown into the fire and burned."

To some this verse means that Christians may fall from grace by not abiding in Christ or by separating from him. As a result, they will be destroyed like the branches.

But this is not in harmony with the whole thrust of what Jesus is saying. On the contrary, the passage is a plea for the disciples to remain in him in order to receive power to bear fruit. Without him, they cannot do this.

They will be like the useless branches that are gathered and burned.

The main point here is that the branches are useless, not that they are destroyed. Scholars constantly warn against treating parables as allegories and pressing each detail for a meaning. While this may make for good devotionalizing, it is bad interpretation. The vine and branches are a kind of parable with one central point: a branch must draw strength from the vine to produce. One should not draw unwarranted conclusions.

James 5:19-20. "My brethren, if anyone among you wanders from the truth and some one brings him back, let him know that whoever brings back a sinner from the error of his way will save his soul from death and will cover a multitude of sins."

This is a kind of tough verse because it does deal with the need for a Christian to seek out an erring brother and bring him to repentance before he experiences the full consequences of his sin. And nothing we have said in this book should be interpreted as minimizing the consequences of a Christian's sin.

Sin is sin just because it hurts somebody—the sinner or someone else. And sin is therefore very deadly indeed. The only argument of this book is that a Christian's sin will never be so great as to reverse the process of salvation or cause him to lose it altogether. He may retard it and cause great harm in the process as these verses indicate.

But doesn't this verse talk about saving a soul from death? Well, yes and no. The Greek word here is *psyche*, which is often translated "soul," but is also translated "life," or "breath." It would be equally proper to translate the verse "to save a life from death." This could well mean to save him from the deadly result of his sins or it could mean even to save him from physical death. First Corinthians 11:30 is interpreted by some to mean that Paul believed that Christians might die earlier than otherwise because of their sins.

As a working pastor, I certainly feel that one who can bring back a straying Christian from his sin has indeed rescued a life from shipwreck. Eternal damnation is not at all necessary to take this verse quite seriously.

1 John 5:16-17.   "If any one sees his brother committing what is not a mortal sin, he will ask, and God will give him life for those whose sin is not mortal. There is sin which is mortal; I do not say that one is to pray for that. All wrongdoing is sin, but there is sin which is not mortal."

This "mortal sin" or "sin unto death" gives a lot of people problems, and we shall discuss this a bit more fully in the section on the unpardonable sin. Here it is sufficient to look at what the passage says.

And what it says is that God promises to restore Christian sinners who are prayed for by their brothers. The only exception is for those who may be sinning a "sin unto death" or toward death. But note again exactly what is said. He does not command prayer for one sinning toward death. But neither does he forbid it. The verse very clearly leaves the door open for such a prayer.

Neither does he say that the sin toward death is unforgivable. It is a more serious sin than others, perhaps because it has death as its direction. He does not say exactly what he has in mind and there is no scholarly agreement on this point. Personally, I prefer to think he is talking about those who deny that "Jesus Christ has come in the flesh." (See 1 John 4:1-3.)

Revelation 2:5. "I will come to you and remove your lampstand from its place, unless you repent."

There is no real difficulty here for a doctrine of perseverance, for the reference is to a church and not individual Christians. An unfaithful church ceases to be a church. It may retain the name "church," but it becomes a social club, a philanthropic society, or something else, but it is not a true church. The verse says nothing about individual members.

Revelation 3:5. "He who conquers shall be clad thus in white garments, and I will not blot his name out of the book of life; I will confess his name before my Father and before his angels."

This is a verse of assurance. No one is said to be blotted out of the book of life. On the contrary, this is exactly what will not happen. Furthermore, verse 8 points out that the names are written before the foundation of the world. If a name could be blotted out, it would imply that God made a mistake in so inscribing the name.

In summary, there are indeed many passages which, taken alone, seem to lean toward the idea of losing one's salvation. None of these, however, cannot be explained as having a quite different meaning. More important, none of these is as convincing to me as the passages that affirm the eternal security of the believer.

Notes

1. Herschel H. Hobbs, *Studies in Hebrews* (Nashville: The Sunday School Board, 1954), pp. 52-57.

4
The Historical and Denominational Positions

The question of perseverance and apostasy is not a new problem. It goes back to the early days of the church and continues. It is instructive to see how the difficulty arose and how it has been handled by various people.

Historical Summary

1. Beginnings of Controversy

While the New Testament makes references to heretics and the dangers of following them, the first time apostasy comes up clearly as a practical matter in church history is somewhat later. Persecution raised the issue.

When the Roman emperors oppressed Christianity, many people's lives were at stake. Many of these stood fast and professed Christ. Some lost their lives. Others went to jail. Still others took the easy way out and either denied Christ or worshiped Caesar as a god. Some of these gave up the faith altogether. But others remained secret Christians or came back after the persecution.

"After all," they reasoned, "isn't it just as well to go through the motions of Caesar-worship and live to be of service to God? Shucks, most of the Romans burn incense to Caesar as a patriotic act, but they don't really think he's a god."

On the other hand, those who had died or been imprisoned were heroes. They were called "witnesses" (or "martyrs" which means "witness" in Greek), and some of these were even now leading the church. This meant there were three classes of members. At the top were the martyrs. Next were the average members who for some reason had not had their faith put to the test. Then there were those who, like Peter, had denied the faith under pressure. What was to be done?

As might be expected, there was a difference of opinion even among the martyrs. Some were for forgiveness; others for excommunications; a third group for discipline or probation.

Out of this setting arose the theological discussion of whether those who had denied Christ had lost their salvation. Very soon a real controversy had flared with some taking this side and some that. The sterner side seems generally to have won out, but it's difficult to say what may have happened in the many scattered churches. By the time the first people involved had died out, the argument had broadened.

What about anyone who sinned? If you sinned after conversion could you lose your salvation? For many people of that day, baptism was necessary to salvation. Indeed, it seemed that almost all the cleansing power of God was focused in that act. One group arose that believed that a real Christian did not sin and if he did he was lost because he could not be rebaptized. So, in some places there developed the practice of postponing baptism as long as possible so that any possible sin might be covered. The ideal was to be baptized just before you died, lying on your deathbed.

2. *Augustine of Hippo*

Augustine was born in A.D. 354. As a young man he had a remarkable conversion experience from paganism and went on to become a bishop of the developing Roman Catholic Church. His thought and writings have had a tremendous influence on theology, even in (I could almost say *especially* in) Protestant churches.

Regarding perseverance, Augustine is a bit of a puzzle. He believed firmly in predestination and that God elected a certain number to be saved. It is frequently thought and stated that those in the line of Augustine and Calvin must also believe in perseverance.

Augustine, however, resists both consistency and being put in categories. (Most great theologians do. What naturally follows, doesn't always.) He believed in predestination, but he did not feel you could know for sure whether you were among the elect until you either got to heaven or didn't. In addition to election, God has to add the grace of perseverance.

On the other hand, Augustine said: "Since they will not in fact persevere unless they both can and will . . . their will is so kindled by the Holy Spirit that they can, just because they will, and they will just because God works in them so to will." [1] Deciphering this, it seems to say that anyone who wants to can persevere and God makes everyone want to!

Perhaps Augustine's position might be summed up by saying that he laid a good groundwork for perseverance, but he was never quite sure about it. Many, but not all, of those who follow his line of thought, go on to affirm perseverance.

3. *Martin Luther*

Nearly everyone knows Luther's famous statement:
"Here I stand. I can do no other. God help me." Everyone
knows also that he launched the Protestant Reformation.

Like Augustine, Luther had a tremendous personal,
spiritual experience. Having tried through years of good
works, self-discipline, and sacrifice to feel that he was
clean before God, Luther finally made the momentous
discovery that God gives salvation by grace alone. Man
does not earn it.

Through a sequence of events, Luther was pushed out
of the Catholic Church and founded both the Reformation
and the denomination we call Lutheran. He had a stormy,
controversial life in and out of the Roman Church. In
fighting heretics on the right and the left, he seems to
have believed that one could indeed lose his salvation.

His followers, along with those of the Arminian school,
have generally taught that "those who were once justified
and regenerated may, by neglecting grace and grieving
the Holy Spirit, fall into such sins as are inconsistent with
true justifying faith, and, continuing and dying in the
same may finally fall into perdition." [2]

4. *The Council of Trent*

To combat the spreading Reformation, the Roman
Catholic Church called a general council which met at
Trent. After much discussion, the council took official
positions on a number of issues. Those positions were
then expressed as official dogma or teachings of the Catholic Church. Anyone who, thereafter, believed or taught
against any of those positions was subject to discipline

and excommunication. Of special interest in our study are these beliefs condemned by the council:

"15. that a man reborn and justified is bound by faith to believe that he is assuredly in the number of the predestinate.

"16. that a man once justified can no more sin, nor can he lose the grace, and so he that falls into sin was never truly justified." [3]

The council thus denied both predestination and perseverance, while also taking a swipe at what we today call Holiness views.

5. John Calvin

Calvin is the man in whom the doctrines of predestination and perseverance reach their fullest and clearest expressions. He was the leader of the French reformation, and from his work grew the Presbyterian and Reformed churches. Since many English Baptists came out of this tradition, Baptists even today are heavily influenced by Calvin's theology. Calvin's views are summed up in the Westminster Confession of Faith of 1643. This very important document is the theological basis of Presbyterianism and has influenced Baptist confessions of faith.

Calvin believed that man's final destiny was chosen by God. He chooses some for salvation and leaves the rest to reprobation (damnation). The reason for God's choices are not clear and cannot be understood by man. The resultant problem can be relieved somewhat by the doctrine of foreknowledge, that God predestined men on the basis of what he knew of them ahead of time.

He went on to say that because Christians were predestined, they must of necessity be eternally secure, always saved. Any who fell by the wayside were never genuine Christians but only those who made a pretense of being a believer. "The elect will endure to the end. The rest are superficial professors."

6. Jacob Arminius

Arminius and his followers moved away from Calvinism in several important respects. While he believed in some type of predestination, Arminius emphasized fore-knowledge as the basis of God's choice. Further, Calvin had taught that God's grace was irresistible—if a man was chosen to be saved, he must be saved. Arminius believed that man could resist the grace of God.

On perseverance he was not dogmatic. He believed that if man did persevere, it had to be by the grace of God and not his own efforts. He felt, however, that it might be possible for man through sloth and negligence to lose his salvation and that at least room should be left open to inquire into this as a real possibility.

Although some Baptist theologians would not agree with Arminius, his position would be generally agreeable to most of the laity today and a good many ministers.

7. The London Confession

While Baptists do not believe in creeds, they do make confessions of faith from time to time. A confession differs from a creed in that the former is simply a statement of what one particular group believes at that time. It is not binding as a creed generally is, nor does it demand that all Baptists agree with its statements.

One of the earliest Baptist confessions of faith was drawn by seven congregations in London in the year 1646.

It has been influential in the shaping of most Baptist confessional statements since then and contains this sentence: "All those that have this precious faith wrought in them by the Spirit can never finally nor totally fall away." To me, this is one of the best ways to set forth the doctrine of perseverance.

Denominational Positions

As might be expected, the treatment of apostasy varies from denomination to denomination. Four groups are here discussed which will cover the ideas of most other churches. It must also be remembered that in most cases there is some variation within the denomination. Perseverance or apostasy is not usually considered a major test of faith, so some members or even leaders may vary from the general position discussed here.

1. Roman Catholics

The Catholic view of salvation is quite different from most Protestants, so the question of perseverance doesn't really come up in the same way at all. For the Roman Catholic, one's final destiny is not settled until life is over and perhaps not until in the afterlife.

Salvation in this system may be compared to a ledger sheet. On one side of the sheet are entered some basic requirements, such as baptism, church membership, the Lord's Supper (Mass). Also entered on that side of the sheet are the good deeds that a person does in life. On the other side of the ledger are the sins a person commits; they are in a sense subtracted from the good deeds. When a person dies, all of his sins must be accounted for before he can enter heaven. They may have been forgiven through confession and penance. Perhaps they may be counterbalanced by good works. Any sins left, however, must be personally atoned for, and this is done through purgatory, a temporary place of punishment.

Thus, apostasy cannot be the same thing for most Catholics as for Protestant evangelicals. Salvation has never been a possession for them, only a goal. So if you drop out along the way, you lose the benefits of the church. Perhaps you may still make it to heaven after a very long time in purgatory. Perhaps not.

Incidentally, a good many Protestants think like this in what might be called folk theology: If I'm a good boy, St. Peter will let me in the golden gates. If I'm a bad boy, I'll go down below. Although rather crude, this is far more Catholic than Protestant.

2. Holiness Groups

A distinction should be made at the outset between Holiness and Pentecostal groups. Some churches are both, but Pentecostal refers to speaking in tongues, and many of these believe you must have this experience to be saved. A Holiness church, however, believes that a Christian is holy in the sense that he does not sin. Many of their people maintain that they do not sin. They feel they may make mistakes and undergo temptation, but do not sin.

To support this they quote such passages as 1 John 3:6: "No one who abides in him sins; no one who sins has either seen him or known him." This does sound pretty clear, but John has just said in the first chapter that "he who says he is without sin is a liar and the truth is not in him." He goes on to say that if we confess our sins, God is faithful and just to forgive us.

The Greek tenses help us out here. A careful study shows that the Christian does not sin in the sense of living a continual life of sin. He does not go on sinning. Rather his sins are isolated acts that are deviations from the whole direction of his life. John is saying that these acts of sin may be forgiven, but anyone whose whole life is aimed away from God is not likely to be a Christian.

Nevertheless, the Holiness people believe they do not sin in any sense of the word. If a Christian does sin, he loses his salvation and must repent and be saved again. This can result (in the extreme) in a saved-lost-saved-lost cycle, and whether one makes it to heaven depends on the state of his soul at the time he dies.

For a Holiness church, then, apostasy is quite possible and very easy compared to the beliefs of other groups. As a practical matter, there are a good many members of these churches who don't really believe this doctrine just as there are Baptists and Presbyterians that believe you can fall from grace.

3. *Mainstream Protestants Who Believe in Apostasy*

Probably the bulk of churches and people belong in this category, and it is very difficult to make a general statement about their beliefs. They definitely do believe you can lose your salvation, but there is no clear-cut agreement as to just how. There are several possibilities.

Some believe the commission of a gross sin like murder or adultery would cause someone to be lost again. A few doubt whether such could ever be saved.

Some feel you could be lost by slowly drifting away from God and the church until at some point you find yourself outside the Kingdom.

A variation of the above is that salvation can be lost through the accumulation of numerous sins of lesser consequence without repenting or asking forgiveness.

Perhaps the largest number of these people think you can lose salvation through a deliberate rejection of Christ and turning your back on the faith.

Almost all who believe in one of these views also think you can be reinstated by God if you confess your sin in a truly penitent manner. They worry about what happens to a person who dies with unconfessed sin.

4. *The Baptist-Presbyterian Position*

This is what we've been talking about all along. We are tempted to call it the New Testament position, since this is what we feel it is. Many members do not understand it, and some do not believe it. Yet it is the "official" position of these denominations. Simply stated, it is that if a person is a Christian, he will never be lost.

All true believers endure to the end. Those whom God has accepted in Christ, and sanctified by His Spirit, will never fall away from the state of grace, but shall persevere to the end. Believers may fall into sin through neglect and temptation, whereby they grieve the Spirit, impair their graces and comforts, bring reproach on the cause of Christ and temporal judgments on themselves, yet God shall keep them by grace through faith unto salvation.

Notes

1. Henry Bettenson, ed., *Documents of the Christian Church* (New York: Oxford University Press, 1956), p. 78.

2. James Hastings, *Encyclopedia of Religion and Ethics* (New York: Charles Scribner's Sons), Vol. 9, p. 769.

3. Bettenson, *op. cit.*, p. 369.

5
Theological Discussion

Theological discussion takes place on several levels. It begins in folk theology—the language of the street. "If you're good, St. Peter will let you in the golden gates."

Next, there is the level of preaching and teaching. At its best, it interprets the Bible and the gospel in the language of the people.

The third level is that of biblical theology. Chapter 2 of this book borders on this area. It is an attempt to discuss an issue in terms of what the Bible says and to think about the issue as the biblical writers would think. A serious discussion of the biblical understanding of covenant would be another example.

This chapter moves into a fourth area, that of systematic theology. In this area man establishes his own categories and tries to fit his understanding of the Bible into them. It is also an effort to ask and answer questions that the Bible does not directly deal with. A good deal of deduction and logic may come into play here in an attempt to develop a system of thought that ties many ideas together. While biblical theology tries to transport modern man back two thousand years to think like a first-century man, systematic theology tries to translate first-century ideas into twentieth-century modes of reason and expression.

There is a fifth level that we shall not be concerned

with in this book but that should be mentioned for completeness. This is the area of philosophical-theology and apologetics. Generally, this area is of interest only to those of special background and training. It is an effort to translate the Bible and theology into universal categories.

The Case for Perseverance

1. Remember the biblical discussion.

We have said we are now approaching the issue theologically, but this does not mean we are deserting the Bible. On the contrary, we deliberately began with the Bible to gain its teaching and should return to the Bible to test the results of our theological efforts.

While there were certain problem passages in the Scriptures, on the whole it seems to teach "once-saved-always-saved." But we noted also that no passage seemed to deal directly with the answer to this question. Nowhere do we find a writer saying anything like, "What then, can a saved man ever again be lost? Why ask you this, for it is plain that . . ." Thus the very question arises in the modern mind more than the ancient mind. In one sense, then, it is basically a matter of asking the Bible questions it does not ask of itself.

We do feel, however, that we have biblical support. What other arguments can we discover?

2. If we could be lost again, we would be persevering by works, whereas we were saved by faith. We are changing the rules.

This is the substance of our biblical argument on Galatians 3. It begins with the evangelical understanding that we are saved by grace through faith and not by works (Eph. 2:8-9). We do not in any sense earn our salvation:

either in the Jewish sense of following the law; the Catholic sense of piling up merits; or the popular sense of doing good deeds. Rather, we are saved entirely by the power of God through grace and faith—two sides of the same coin.

Grace is God's side of the coin. It means undeserved favor. While we were yet sinners, Christ died for us. Not only do we not earn salvation, we very definitely do not even deserve it. God saves us *in spite of our sin.*

Faith is man's side of the coin. It is our response to grace. It is not really an active thing. It is simply accepting God's offer of salvation. In a very real sense every man is already saved, in that the price for his sin has been paid on Calvary. Yet, not every man accepts that price. It is rather like a store telephoning to say you have a gift someone has left there for you to pick up. It is yours, but you must go get it. If you don't, you don't have it.

Taken together, grace and faith may be pictured as a marriage ceremony. The officiant says, "Do you claim this human as your child?" And God says, "I do." (That's grace.) Then the officiant asks, "And do you accept the Lord as your God?" And you say, "I do." (That's faith.)

Now, if this is the way we are saved, does it make sense all of a sudden to change the rules? Are we to say: "Now God has forgiven us of our past sins and given us a fresh start. From here on out, however, we must carry on largely on our own strength. Grace can only go so far. Now works take over"? As Paul was fond of saying in graphic Greek, *"Me Genoito"*—God forbid! Let it not be so! By no means! No way!

Rather, if God was so gracious to us while we were still sinners, how much more, now that we are his children, will he be anxious to forgive us and carry us on in his strength (cf. Rom. 5:8 ff).

The Roman Catholics are at least consistent. They believe you must work (among other things) for salvation, and it is reasonable for them to believe that you must continue to work (again, among other things) to retain it. But if we believe that salvation is not of works at the beginning, consistency demands that we not change the rules. Beginning in grace, we end in grace. God saves us and God keeps us.

3. If we could be lost again, Christ is ineffective as Savior.

Apostasy, at least as carried in the popular mind, comes very close to insulting God. If a person could be saved and then lost, it would appear that Christ does a better job of saving some than others. Now it is obvious that there are varying levels of commitment; some follow closely; some follow farther off; and some stray. But to say they are lost?

Now we must remember what we pointed out in Chapter 1—that the New Testament describes salvation as a pretty drastic experience. It completely remakes a person. It talks about being born again, new creatures, and all of this. In short, it speaks of a glorious and transforming experience. How complete would this experience be if it could be so easily lost?

At the popular and preaching level, a point is worthy of notice. Many preachers like to say that falling from grace would be the same thing as being un-born. In the physical realm this is impossible. Many things may happen to a person. He may die. But he cannot be un-born. He has physical existence in time and space. Likewise in the spiritual realm, if a man is born again, he cannot become un-born. He has forever a spiritual existence in God's time and space.

In short, there are far less problems with our ideas of God's grace and Christ's power as Savior if we accept that he does the job right the first time—once and for all.

4. If apostasy were possible, how many or what kind of sins would be required?

One good way to understand an issue is to ask what would happen if the opposite were true. In this case, what would be the situation if a person could be lost after having been saved? What exactly would he have to do to lose his salvation?

Here the Holiness people are consistent. Any sin (at least for many of these people) causes you to be lost again. After all, the same God who said not to kill also said not to steal. Thus if you do not murder anyone but take a washcloth from a hotel, you have sinned and so lost your salvation because a Christian does not sin.

Of course, most Christians feel this is not the way it is. Minor sins will not lose your salvation for you. Neither will unconscious sins or unknowing sins. Big deliberate sins like murder or adultery might.

But where do you draw the line? If this were so, I should think the Bible would be quite clear and list which were big sins and which were little. It doesn't do that. Indeed, it's hard for anyone to do that. Just try it, and before long you find yourself talking like the Pharisees with whom even Jesus lost patience.

What is an unconscious sin? Psychiatrists aren't sure what the unconscious is. What is an unknowing sin? Could

you perhaps be guilty because if you had applied yourself
to your Bible a bit more, you would have recognized
that it was a sin? Which is bigger: the adulterer or the
gossip who publicizes the guilt and so may shut off the
adulterer's escape routes? What's a big sin? What's a little
sin? I'm not sure I know. Maybe you do.

There are some who feel that apostasy is perhaps
limited to a deliberate rejection of Christ. Thus, one could
lose his salvation if he consciously and willfully rejects
both Jesus and his salvation. I feel this is a better position
than most, and if one feels he must believe in falling
from grace, this is the most satisfactory of the choices.
I cannot personally go along with this however, but it
is discussed more fully later.

5. *Does the security of the believer mean you can sin
as you please?*

This is another theological question raised by both
opponents and proponents of perseverance. "Why you
Baptists believe you can be saved and then go out and
sin all you want to." Well, judging by their actions, some
Baptists apparently do believe that, but this is not really
what we are advocating. And yet, in another sense, this
is what we are advocating.

If you emphasize the word "saved" as we did in Chapter
1, you almost can say a Christian can sin as much as
he likes without being lost. The point is that a person,
who is a genuine Christian, is not going to have the same
attitude as a non-Christian. If a person is genuinely converted, he will have a different set of desires from the
unconverted, at least much of the time.

The doctrine of perseverance does mean that we do
not use the threat of being lost as a whipping boy to

keep our church members in line. (An exception might be that if one seems *too* wayward or negligent, he might well reexamine his salvation experience.) Our emphasis rather is as Paul's emphasis to the Romans: What then, shall you who have been saved from sin, continue to live as sinners? (See Rom. 6.)

Of course, many people fear that if they believed in perseverance they would not have the strength to avoid sin since they could not be lost. This is certainly a possibility, but I know of no one who has openly taken this stand since the Gnostics, and a good deal of the New Testament is written to refute them. The Scriptures seem to teach that a saved person can never be lost and that even sins after salvation do not change this. It does not go on to say, however, that we may, therefore, continue in sin without fear. Rather, it explicitly points out that this is one of the chief things we are saved from and should by no means continue therein.

An advantage at this point is that we are free to choose our courses of action without being stalemated in fear. We can choose in faith that God will redeem our actions—or at least forgive them.

6. *The doctrine of predestination virtually requires that we believe in perseverance.*

It is no accident that Presbyterians and Baptists, who share a Calvinistic background of predestination, should also share a belief in eternal security. Predestination is the doctrine that God has at least known—and probably called—some people to salvation "from the foundation of the world." Before they were born, God chose them to be Christians. Now this is a very difficult teaching to understand, and it sets off a whole chain of other

questions. Chapter 6 discusses some of these a bit more
for those who are interested.

At this point, however, it is enough to say that the
New Testament is very clear about the *fact* of predestination, whatever it may mean by it. The classic passage
is Romans 8:29-30. "For those whom he foreknew he also
predestined to be conformed to the image of his Son,
in order that he might be the first-born among many
brethren. And those whom he predestined he also called;
and those whom he called he also justified; and those
whom he justified he also glorified." While this passage
may even teach perseverance, it very definitely talks
about foreknowledge and predestination.

Here the deductions of theology come in. If God obviously knows who is going to be saved ahead of time
and calls these to be Christians, there is *no way* these
can be lost without God's knowledge being in error and
his calling and will for these people being thwarted. It
follows that these will just naturally endure to the end.
Otherwise, God's knowledge would be false and his predestination (whatever that is) would be frustrated.

*7. If apostasy were possible, which of the three aspects
of salvation would it affect?*

Now this is where I get in trouble, because I'm going
to admit that I believe in apostasy. I am not, however,
going to admit to believing you can lose your salvation.
I don't believe that's the same thing.

We have divided salvation into three parts: past,
present, and future. It is difficult to see how apostasy
could affect past sins or forgiveness. These are over and
done with.

But it is very hard to deny that apostasy does affect

the present life, more specifically that portion of life between the apostasy and repentance or the grave, which-ever comes first. One thing we have failed to com-municate to the world, both to the lost and to much of the saved, is that the Christian life here and now is the best life. It is not the opiate of the masses nor a rigid trial for the joys of heaven. It is the best way to live life on the earth. It is the most joyful, the most satisfying, the most productive. It is often the most happy.

Conversely, sin is not sin because God dumped the various possible attitudes and actions of man into a hat one day and then pulled them out at random, saying to one "that's OK" and to the next "that's a no-no." Rather, sin is sin because it goes against the fundamental nature of man and the universe. More simply, sin is sin because it hurts somebody. It either hurts the sinner or somebody else. It may hurt now or it may hurt later.

Thus the apostate who backslides into sin is going to lose many of the present benefits of salvation because he is not going to have the best kind of life. If you don't believe me, ask some backsliders who have had a fresh experience with Christ in rededication or renewal. They tell me there is no comparison. Incidentally, very few of these repentant apostates feel the need to be baptized again. They feel they were at one time genuinely saved and never lost that salvation, even though they wandered pretty far astray.

Now, the big question in most people's minds involves the future. We have said you can't lose past salvation, but you can lose some of the present benefits. If you quit paying on an insurance policy, it usually lapses and you may even lose all benefits.

Salvation is not like that. You do not lose future benefits—at least not the big one. You do get into heaven—that's one thing this book is trying to say all the way through. There *is* the very real possibility that you will be short on rewards in the future life. But that's another subject.

What the Bible Means by Apostasy

The word "apostasy" itself is very seldom used in the Bible. The idea, however, is frequently present. If we are to believe that a saved person can never be lost, we must give some kind of positive value to the concept of apostasy. We cannot simply explain how these statements do not mean something, while failing to explain what they in fact do mean. The New Testament has so many warnings and so much to say on the subject that it must mean something. Further, our own experience tells us that people who have at one time lived very religious lives do wander off into flagrant sin and unconcern. This too must be explained.

The word "apostasy" is an English writing of a Greek word which means falling away. It is used only in Hebrews 6:6 (see biblical discussion). In English it has become a loaded word to mean, to many people at any rate, losing their salvation. More strictly, however, it means simply a falling away from something once believed or followed or adhered to.

1. In the Bible "apostasy" sometimes means the falling away of those who never believed.

Jude describes "some who long ago were designated for condemnation, ungodly persons who pervert the grace of our God into licentiousness and deny our only master and Lord, Jesus Christ" (Jude 4). These were apparently passing as Christians, for he says they had secretly gained admission.

This category also includes those in Jesus' parable of the soils who believed for awhile and then fell away when the going got rough or the excitement wore off.

2. *Apostasy sometimes means the infiltration of false teachers.*

The Christian faith was new, and it was vitally important to men like Paul to be sure that what they were doing would last. They were telling men of the good news of the life-giving power they had found in Jesus Christ. Now others began coming with a message that would enslave the people again under the name of freedom. One group taught that you had to earn salvation through doing the works prescribed by the Jewish law. An opposite faction preached that you could accept salvation and still live licentiously since your soul was saved and your body was free to do what it liked.

We must remember that there was no New Testament in those days to use as a standard. Indeed much of the New Testament was written to combat rising heresies and to give a standard by which to measure Christian teachings. Galatians was written to combat the Judaizers who insisted you had to be first a Jew, then a Christian. First John was written perhaps to combat the opposite view of the Greek Gnostics.

It was extremely important in those days to fight for doctrinal purity. If, for example, the Gnostics had won, we would have had a quite different New Testament, if Christianity had survived at all. You can see this if you will read the noncanonical gospels according to

Thomas and Phillip.

For this reason, there was a constant warning against those who came in the name of Christ but were in fact trying to teach a different faith than he taught and the apostles were teaching. This is in the background of many passages dealing with apostasy.

3. Apostasy sometimes means the falling away of a church or a group in its teachings or theology.

This, of course, is related directly to the false teachers. Many of the pleas against apostasy are not so much directed against one person's falling from grace as they are against a church leaving the proper understanding of the faith for a heresy to the right or the left. It is possible that the difficult passages in Hebrews can be understood in this light.

We have also mentioned the letters to the Galatians and that of John. An even clearer instance might be the letters to the seven churches in the first chapters of the book of Revelation. Here the messages are quite clear for the churches to stand fast against all heresy.

4. Apostasy may also mean the backsliding of Christians who thwart, for a time, God's efforts in the present toward growth and service.

Early Christians were by no means perfect, and the New Testament makes this obvious. Indeed, many of them came from a very pagan background and were guilty of what to us would appear very flagrant sins for a Christian. First Corinthians discusses the problem of a very mixed-up church, and in so doing it covers a variety of problems of individual Christians. This is a type of apostasy.

Although it is not called by the name, Simon Peter

commits a real apostasy in his denial of Jesus. Luke 22:31-34 tells of Peter's supreme confidence that he (Peter) will not betray Jesus even if everyone else should. The Lord, in turn, tells him that morning will not come before he is three times a denier. Then Jesus tells Peter that after he has "pulled out of it" (literally: "turned again, repented, converted," etc.) he should strengthen the others. Jesus foresees the apostasy of all the disciples, Simon more than the others. Yet he sees their restoration to faith, Simon first before the others. Jesus further feels that even a denier will have the strength to help other apostates back into service.

This is a beautiful example of Jesus dealing with apostasy, and his faith in the return of those who deny him. If it could happen to Peter, it could happen to us.

5. *Apostasy could mean a conscious decision to reject Christ, somewhat like the conscious decision to accept Christ.*

While I do not believe this personally, this is to me the only rational grounds on which one could hold to a doctrine of falling from grace that would include the total loss of salvation. Some of the passages in Hebrews and Peter could be interpreted this way, while avoiding some of the difficulties. One could add to this a drifting away from Christ to the extent that it amounts to a conscious rejection.

The reasons I don't believe in this can be gathered throughout the book. Basically, it raises more questions than it solves. What would constitute such a decision?

Many youth, for example, when they reach college find themselves ill-prepared to handle all manner of arguments directed against the faith as they have been taught it.

Some of these feel, like Adam and Eve, that they are gaining superior knowledge and so reject the religion they were raised in as the superstition of their parents and the establishment. Most of these come back later with a deepened understanding and their adolescent rebellion behind them. This is intellectual apostasy, and it is usually temporary. It can even be debated as to how much of an apostasy it actually is since most of these kids have not been exposed to a very rigorous grounding in theology or apologetics and have no solid theology to defend.

Others never reject orthodoxy but fall in with the playboy philosophy to "live it up" for a few years. These, too, may settle back into respectable morality and join their parents in sighing over the next generation.

Both groups are temporary apostates. Are we to say that if they die during their apostasy they will be lost but if they die after their return they will be saved? Or are we to say this is merely a temporary sort of aberration and the truly saved will come back?

And there are still more problems. Consider intellectual apostasy. Exactly what constitutes final intellectual apostasy? Which doctrines are crucial in such rejection?

At one time a group arose, the ones first calling themselves Fundamentalists, with five fundamentals of the faith that one had to believe in order to be a Christian. I happened to have studied this group and found that there were in fact *seven* different propositions in the movement, and not all agreed on which five were *the* fundamental propositions. Of course, the Roman Catholic Church solved this sort of difficulty a long time ago by saying that faith involves accepting what the Church declares is true.

This makes of faith more than a personal encounter with Jesus. It demands the good work of intellectual acceptance of certain propositions. A favorite one is the virgin birth of Jesus. Now I believe in this doctrine, but it happens that I recall very clearly the time in my late teens when it suddenly burst on me exactly what this doctrine meant. I had been a Christian for some years.

If a person can be lost for not believing intellectually certain things, it seems to me that the Bible should say this very clearly and give us a list of those propositions along with definitions of critical words. Since the Bible does not do this, I must hold to the idea that a man is saved by a personal encounter with the living Christ, regardless of what beliefs he holds going into or coming out of that experience. Think about Paul on the road to Damascus for a while.

Now if a person can be lost by drifting—just sort of drifting away for years through numerous sins and general negligence of his spiritual life, another problem arises. At just what point does he become lost? On which morning or evening does he lose his salvation?

The Holiness groups are consistent here by saying that one sin makes you lost. Catholics try for some consistency by dividing sins into venial and mortal, those that can be forgiven easily and those that can't. But this has not always worked clearly in practice and is of dubious biblical value.

Pretend for a minute that you can portray a spiritual drift into apostasy by a straight line. At what point on that line has one drifted so far that he cannot get back and so is lost? I don't believe this can happen. I don't believe anyone can ever get so far from the love of God that he cannot be restored, and restored immediately.

Nevertheless, if after studying the Bible—all of it—very carefully, you still feel that it teaches that a saved person can be lost, the only solid way you can take this position would be to make the act of apostasy a very definite and drastic act equivalent to a conversion experience, in reverse.

Reconstruction

Having covered a good deal of ground, it is worth stopping a minute to review and see where we stand. We have seen some advantages from the biblical and theological standpoints. Let us reiterate these here and add some psychological advantages.

1. Biblical advantages. For me, the chief advantage here is that "perseverance" leaves me with less problems of interpretation than "apostasy." There are some problems, and I am aware that the explanations given in Chapter 3 will not convince everyone. On the other hand, the very fact that they appear difficult comes from the fact that they stand out against the rest of the Scriptures as apparent exceptions. The general thrust of the New Testament is that God took the initiative in saving sinners and that by his strength we will persevere.

2. Theological Advantages. Perseverance gives a more consistent theology than apostasy. Without perseverance one is left in a vague sort of state, neither saved nor lost, until one dies. This can only be relieved by some system of merit such as the Catholics teach, or by an all-or-nothing approach such as the Holiness idea.

If you believe that a Christian can fall from grace and so lose his salvation, then redemption is only a future goal and never a present possession. It is something like holding a carrot out before a donkey to make him move. He never gets the carrot until the end of the day's work, if then. The New Testament speaks of salvation as a present possession, however, and not something that hangs in the balance until the end. Indeed salvation may be said to possess *you*.

3. Psychological advantages. I have long suspected that there are a couple of things at issue in this controversy that don't always appear on the surface. Consider the psychological effect of the two opposing positions.

• If one accepts that one may be lost after being saved, this gives God, the church, and the minister a kind of whip to hold over the heads of the members. If you don't fall into line, you won't make it. The Roman Catholic Church has actually spelled this out and threatens to excommunicate members, withdrawing God's grace and salvation from them, if they don't repent of their sin or recant of their heresy.

I suspect that many theologians, ministers, and pastors are afraid that if their people believed in "once-saved-always-saved" they would no longer work for the church and the organizations connected therewith. They would also be likely to fall into sin since "it wouldn't make any difference." So the possibility of losing salvation is used as a disciplinary threat to keep the members in line.

In practice, this does not seem to work much better than the other way. There is no higher percentage of active members in churches that hold to apostasy than in those believing in perseverance.

• If you've got to have a whipping boy, one can always query whether a person has in fact been converted in the first place. If his actions seem to argue against his being a Christian, perhaps he could be challenged to reexamine his conversion experience.

And yet I have found, as a pastor, that very few people who seem after some years to "wake up" as a Christian feel they have just then been saved and should be baptized. Rather, most of these usually testify that they were sincere in their earlier experience but had wandered away. They may rededicate their lives publicly or privately or even begin to live a more open and active Christian life without any obvious decision. All of these seem to do as well as those who request re-baptism because they feel they had never been converted.

• There is a positive advantage to the belief in the security of the believer. It leaves a person free to live the Christian life in confidence. This, indeed, is the meaning of the term "gospel" or good news.

In Galatians 5:13 Paul says "you were called to freedom." The law did not allow a man to be free. He was always afraid lest he be condemned by not obeying some rule. Apostasy puts a man in the same position. For a Christian to be saved from the law and then thrown back into keeping the law to retain his salvation is not very much gain at all.

• Incidentally, it should be noted that we sometimes change the law, substituting the modern law for that of the Old Testament, a dubious improvement. We equate falling from grace with failing to attend, contribute, participate, or accept responsibility in the organizational church. We may likewise imply that if one does not fall into line with this law as promoted by the preachers (often inscribed on envelopes and paper attendance slips rather than stone) then one has lost his salvation.

This is bad business indeed. Either invoke the law both for salvation and perseverance or omit it all together. Do not import the law after salvation as a shyster lawyer reveals the fine print after the contract is signed.

• Perseverance shows confidence in the individual on two counts. First, because God has created him and so has a unique plan for his life. This was laid out before the foundation of the world. Second, because God has redeemed him and is now at work in his life helping him to develop and use his abilities in accordance with God's design.

This can give confidence for Christian living. Sin does not have a devastating effect any longer, for it may be forgiven and life resumed. It becomes a temporary check rather than a checkmate or even a threatened mate. There are few things more exhilarating to the spirit than to be able to live, secure in the knowledge that God is for us and nothing can be against us.

The Value of the Doctrine of Perseverance

What good is all this anyway? Why take all this time and effort over this question? There are those who brush off this topic as a question of minor interest, so let us suggest several values of this study, some of which have been already implied.

1. It answers a question. A great deal of theology evolved in answer to questions. When man asks a question, it is reasonable to answer it if the answer is available in the present state of man's knowledge. If not readily available, it is reasonable to try to discover or deduce an answer if time taken in this project does not destroy a more productive use of time.

2. *It emphasizes the nature of salvation.* You can't talk about keeping something unless you know what it is you are keeping. Therefore an inquiry into keeping salvation must begin with the question of what salvation is in the first place. And this is one of the most basic doctrines in the faith. Studying related teachings throws light on the central ones. In this case, we have discovered that salvation is a more far-reaching and life-changing event than we often recognize.

3. *It suggests proper approaches to backsliders.* In other words, you don't threaten them with loss of salvation if they don't come back to church. Rather, you assume one of two things: either they have never been converted or that God is still trying to work in their lives. If the latter is true, you may be sure that approaching another as a Christian brother with sins only slightly different from your own will get further than a judgmental or warning attitude.

4. *It gives security to the Christian and freedom to live.* This has been discussed above under "Psychological Advantages," but it is important enough to underline by mentioning again. The Christian faith gives man freedom from all sorts of things: from his own past with its sins and mistakes, from fear of the future including his own death, from fear of the present and his inadequacies.

It frees him, and freeing him enables him to relax, enjoy life, and love. For some reason where the Spirit of God is there is freedom, and where freedom is, love comes. Man is more likely to serve God and serve him well when he is set free and told he is free than when he is threatened. Stand fast, therefore, in that freedom wherewith Christ has set you free.

6
Some Related Issues

One of the nice things about the Bible and theological discussion generally is that one exploration leads to another. Of course, this can be a nuisance at times, such as when you must go back and study gnosticism to understand more fully what 1 John is all about. In this study we have uncovered a few other interesting subjects which might help in better understanding the preceding pages. So this chapter is devoted to discussing them more fully than could be done before. By no means think, however, that these brief summaries exhaust these subjects.

How Can I Know If I Am Saved?

Almost every Christian asks this at one time or another. People who are not Christians ask it. In one way, it may be answered very simply, and yet at times it can be frustratingly difficult to answer. Let's begin with the simple answer.

1. The Easy Answer

You are saved if you have trusted or are trusting in Jesus Christ to save you. Other ways to express "trust" are: "believe in," "surrender to," "commit yourself to," "follow as a disciple."

The Bible is quite clear on this. "He who believes in him is not condemned; he who does not believe is condemned already" (John 3:18).

Sometimes the New Testament will add other things in talking about belief because these almost always follow when a person begins a life of faith. This includes repentance, baptism, public confession, and the like. But if these were *the* essential, they would always be mentioned rather than only here and there. The only thing always required is faith, expressed in one form or another.

If you believe, you are saved.

2. The More Difficult Answer

Often our problem is more of a psychological one. We are really asking something like this: If I died right now, can I be absolutely sure that I will not cease to exist or go to hell, but rather that I will continue as myself in a happy state of existence that we call heaven? This is linked to a further question about the past: Have I done the proper thing to insure the future?

Now the way out of this for a person without any undue psychological problems is to do one of two things. First, re-read the section above. Then ask yourself if you have believed. If so, you're OK.

Second, if this still troubles you, move the question from the past and the future into the present which is a better place to handle it anyway. Regardless of what you did or didn't do in the past, are you right now trying to follow Christ? If so, you're OK. If not, get with it.

Some people have an extra problem here, depending on their psychological bent. They just can't seem to shake this doubt, and many go through a period of life when this question troubles them exceedingly. Occasionally you will find someone being re-baptized, perhaps even two or three times, to try to feel clear in his mind about this. He may have talked to a number of preachers.

When this happens, very likely the problem is not first of all a spiritual one, but a psychological one. It is a kind of obsession that can't be whipped—or so it seems.

If you happen to be in this condition, check first of all to see if you're under a lot of temporary strain. Have you just started college or taken a new job? Got married or had a new baby? Have you had a recent grief or financial loss? Have you some weight of sin or guilt that is troubling you? If so, you should in all likelihood deal with this first, then return to the salvation question. Give yourself time to get adjusted to the new situation. If simply asking God to forgive you of your sin does not relieve the problem, find someone you can talk with about it who will still love you and keep his mouth shut. Then return to the question of salvation.

The doctrine of perseverance will be of help here. Perhaps you could say (as I've heard some say) that I know once I was a Christian, but I'm not sure now. Well friend, if this book makes sense, you can simply trust God to be faithful to you and keep what you have entrusted to him while you are working out your other difficulties. Indeed, he himself will be working in you and with you to transform your present situation into what he wants it to be.

Even after all this, someone may still feel he just can't get completely satisfied that he is saved. He is deeply troubled about his salvation and has tried many things without success. He has discussed it with a half dozen or more preachers, he has made numerous public decisions, he has done what Billy Graham says, he has tried

to believe, and yet there is still that troublesome doubt
gnawing away. He may find it hard to work for worrying
about it.

If so, he needs a dependable counselor who will discuss
this matter with him regularly for a period of time. If
he reads these lines, let me say to him: "You do not need
to live forever in that kind of misery. If it troubles you
that much, you almost certainly are saved, for God will
never turn down one who has searched for him as ear-
nestly as you have. Seek a pastor who is trained in coun-
seling or find an understanding doctor or psychologist.
Don't be afraid to try a psychiatrist or a mental health
clinic. Once you get this mental roadblock out of the
way, the spiritual problem disappears as if by magic."

What Is the Unpardonable Sin?

First John 5:16 says: "There is sin which is mortal;
I do not say that one is to pray for that." (But note he
does not forbid it either.)

Mark 3:28-29 says: "All sins will be forgiven the sons
of men and whatever blasphemies they utter; but whoever
blasphemes against the Holy Spirit never has forgiveness,
but is guilty of an eternal sin" (cf. Matt. 12:31-32).

First, let me see if I can put your mind at rest. If
you're worrying about having committed the unpardonable sin, you haven't. If you had committed it, you wouldn't
know it nor worry about it. You may not even believe
in sin if you had committed this one!

Most Bible scholars today believe that the unforgivable
sin is to become so hardened in heart that you attribute
the works of God to the work of the devil and vice versa.
Thus you reject the call of God to follow Christ as an

evil call and deliberately follow evil, believing it to be good.

This is a purely spiritual sin. It is not an act or deed committed by man. Specifically, it is *not* a sexual sin in spite of the fact that many people feel they can't be forgiven after having committed a sexual sin.

The unpardonable sin is a flat rejection of God's power in the Spirit. This is admittedly mysterious. In Luke, Jesus expounds that you can blaspheme God or Christ, but not the Spirit. It seems this is a particularly hard condition of the soul where one attributes the work of God to the devil or to some evil source.

This is borne out by the context in Mark. The Pharisees have just said that Jesus is healing by the power of Beelzebub. In other words, they are saying Jesus is inspired by the devil, possessed by an evil spirit instead of empowered by the Holy Spirit. Thus, these men are not only blaspheming against Jesus, but against the Power that moves him. This is unforgivable since they do not recognize God in order to turn to him.

What Does Predestination Mean?

This is a tough one.

Let's begin on a happy note by saying that in the New Testament predestination is always considered as a glorious comfort and never as a problem. The emphasis is that we can never be defeated because we are part of the eternal plan of God. We have been chosen since before the world began, or at least before *we* began.

The classic passage is Romans 8:29-30. "For those whom he foreknew he also predestined to be conformed to the image of his Son, in order that he might be the first-born among many brethren. And those whom he predestined he also called; and those whom he called he also justified; and those whom he justified he also glorified." Other passages reinforce this.

Now what do they mean?

Briefly, predestination means that God has picked out some people ahead of time to be saved. He has elected them. Now, the problem arises as to why he picked out some. Or, more exactly, why he left out some. (There are a few extremists who believe in "double-barreled" predestination, i.e., God not only elected some to be saved, but some to go to hell. Most folks don't go that far, and—as we mentioned—the Bible only speaks positively and triumphantly on this point.)

Paul ties this in with foreknowledge. Those whom he foreknew, he predestinated. This relieves the problem for a lot of people. We still have freedom of choice—God merely sealed our decision ahead of time, knowing what that decision would be.

And freedom of choice is the real issue. We want to feel free to choose our own destinies. It is ironic that we are so concerned about our own freedom that we don't want to give God the same freedom. I believe that one way of looking at predestination is to consider it as a statement of God's freedom. God does not have to accept any man. No act of ours, not even an act of faith, *compels* God to save us. He remains free to choose us as we are to choose him. Predestination is one way of preventing us from commanding God how he must act.

Then let's look at the matter of time a little more closely. Time does not mean to God what it does to us. We can picture God as sitting outside the world and universe and watching it. We can also imagine God sitting outside of time and "watching" it. After all, he created time as well as space. He is simultaneously in the past and future. All time is open to him as the rooms of a house might be open to us. Thus, for him to predestinate is as much a present and future act as a past act. Someone has likened it to sitting in a tower watching a parade. On the street one sees only the part passing by in front. From the tower both the beginning and end can be seen.

Adding to this the idea discussed previously of the covenant, it says to me that our salvation is a free act on God's part and a relatively free act on my part. It is a voluntary entering into a contract, similar in many ways to a marriage contract. And yet God is the major party. He has swept me off my feet. He has come to me in grace that is almost irresistible, calling me to follow. And I have said yes. And yet, I was free to say no.

Perhaps this brief sketch of a doctrine even more complicated than perseverance will be of some help. It can at least point to one real source of assurance that once we are saved, we are always saved since we are a part of God's eternal plan.

What About the Holiness Doctrines?

We have said that many Holiness people solve this problem by saying that the true Christian never sins. If you do sin, you fall from grace and cease to be a Christian. You need to be saved all over again.

Most Christians I know—even some who belong to the Holiness denominations—do not go along with this teaching. They are well enough aware from their own experience that they sin daily and stand constantly in need of forgiveness. Indeed, it is one of the paradoxes of Christian growth that the more you grow in understanding and maturity, the more conscious you are of your sins. The closer you are to Christ, the more you are aware of how far you are from Christ.

And yet the Bible makes what seem to be very clear statements that Christians do not sin, especially in 1 John. This troubles us. And yet the entire book of 1 John is written to Christians. And it is to them that the writer also says very clearly that if we say we have no sin, we lie and do not the truth. But if we confess our sins, he is faithful and just to forgive us our sins and to cleanse us from all iniquity (see 1 John 1:8-9).

Now if John very clearly says we do sin and should ask forgiveness, he must have some other meaning when he says we don't sin. And what he means is simply this: we do not continue in a regular walk in the paths of sin. We do not live as though nothing had happened to us. The direction of our lives is changed. Whereas we may stray from the path now and then, at least we are now on the right path.

There is some debate as to whether Romans 7 is a reference to Paul's life before or after conversion. Personally, I think it is a post-conversion passage because I doubt he had this same type of soul-struggle as a sanctimonious Pharisee. Nevertheless, it strikes true to the experience of many Christians who are trying to follow the teachings of Christ. We are indeed in a struggle with sin, but it is a struggle we shall win because we no longer belong to sin, but to God.

Should We Expect Rewards?

I want to say a brief word about rewards since this concept relieves at least some problems connected with perseverance. If we all are going to persevere, what difference does it make what kind of life we lead? One answer is that we shall receive rewards in heaven in proportion to our works on earth.

This is a biblical doctrine. Not a great deal is said, however, about what the rewards are, merely that there will be rewards. Jesus refers to these several times in the Sermon on the Mount: Matthew 5:12,19-20; 6:1, 4,6,18-21. There are many other references to rewards throughout the Bible, and these include both earthly and heavenly rewards. One other reference that particularly fascinates me is the parable of the talents in Matthew 25:14 ff. In this parable the rewards are greater responsibility to the man who is faithful in using what he has. The setting in the discussion leaves room for this to apply in a future life as well as this life.

This concept of rewards, along with threats of punishment that apply to all sin, can ease somewhat the fear that a man once saved will feel free to sin if he knows he cannot be lost. On the other hand, there are two other aspects to the question of rewards.

First, we must not translate material rewards from earth to heaven. It is not fair to say that God will not reward us materially here and then picture heavenly rewards as a luxurious and materialistic earthly life. We can become pretty crass about heaven if we're not careful.

Second, we must always recognize that we *have* received our greatest reward already in the forgiveness of sin and the redemption for eternity. Nothing can match this, for salvation is the greatest possible reward.

Must a Baptist Believe in Perseverance?

No.

Many Baptists don't. Most don't even understand the

doctrine, much less believe in it. Some don't even know there is such a thing. Some are "good, solid, orthodox Baptists" (whatever this means) in every other respect but can't agree on this.

One of the greatest parts of our Baptist heritage is that we do not have a creed. You do not have to sign anything to be a Baptist. We have emphatically rejected creeds throughout our history. There have been those who tried to get us to adopt creeds—there still are. Some get up in arms about modernists and liberals that will creep in and destroy the faith. So they want some kind of creed or statement of faith signed by (at least) key leaders. The irony of all this is that the denominations who have had creeds have been far more heavily influenced by liberals than have Baptists without one.

Why is this so?

Because we have emphasized the Bible as the center. No creed but the Bible. And each individual Christian has the right to interpret the Bible for himself with the aid of the Holy Spirit.

So if we do not see eye to eye on this or any other matter, I shall not try to throw you out, and I trust you will try to tolerate me. Rather, I shall pray that God will reveal even this to you, i.e., that he will persuade you—or perchance even me.

God himself will prove perseverance when he gathers us to himself.

P.S. You don't have to be a Baptist or Presbyterian to
      believe in perseverance!